AF425265

# BANKING

# AND

# INSURANC

## About the Author

Dr. Mohammad Iqbal Dar often incorporates his latest research findings into his lectures, ensuring that students are exposed to current advancements and understand how theoretical knowledge can be applied practically.

Dr. Monika Agarwal has a knack for deconstructing complicated concepts into simpler, digestible parts, making her courses highly inclusive and beneficial for students from diverse backgrounds.

Dr. Sajad Ahmad Mir is known for encouraging critical thinking and open discussions in the classroom, fostering an environment where students learn to question and innovate.

## Copyright Certificate

This is to certify that the intellectual property contained in the work produced by:

**Dr. Mohammad Iqbal Dar**

**Dr. Monika Agarwal**

**Dr. Sajad Ahmad Mir**

is the exclusive property of the respective authors All rights, including but not limited to reproduction, distribution, public performance, and creation of derivative works, are reserved under applicable copyright laws.

Any unauthorized use, reproduction, or distribution of the aforementioned work(s) is strictly prohibited without the express written consent of the authors.

Issued on: [22-10-2022]

Location: [India]

| Group | Course outlines |
|---|---|
| Group-A | Bank Meaning Importance, Banker – Customer Relationship definition and meaning of Banker &Customer, permitted activities of Commercial Banks in India – General & Special features of their relationship – Rights & Duties. |
| | Deposit Accounts – Opening operations and closure of fixed deposit accounts, recurring account, Savings Account, Current and Deposit Schemes for N.R.I's. |
| Group-B | Banking Investments – Negotiable instruments (NI) – Types parties to NI's – Crossing, Endorsements, Payments and Collection of Cheques, Bouncing of Cheques – Implications, various laws affecting bankers. |
| | Banking Services – Safe custody, MICR clearing, ATM's, Credit Cards, Debit Cards, Travelling Cheques, Ombudsman and Customer services, Fraud Detection and control. |
| Group-C | Emerging Trends and Issues – International banking, Euro Banks and Offshore Banking, overview of Banking risks, Corporate governance, Credit Risk Management in Banks – Liquidity Risk Management – Asset Liability Management. |
| Group-D | Insurance, Meaning types scope importance. Governing agencies, LIC. Fire and marine Insurance. Agriculture Insurance Brief history of insurance in India |

**INDEX**

## CHAPTER 1

**BANKING AND CUSTOMER RELATIONSHIP**

Definition of Banking

Finance is the life blood of trade, commerce and industry. Now-a-days, banking sector acts as the backbone of modern business. Development of any country mainly depends upon the development of its banking system. The term bank is either derived from Old Italian word banca or from a French word banque both mean a Bench or money exchange table. In olden days, European money lenders or money changers used to display (show) coins of different countries in big heaps (quantity) on benches or tables for the purpose of lending or exchanging.

Bank's definition as per Banking Regulation Act 1949:

According to Section 5(b) of Banking Regulation Act, 1949 (BR Act) the business of Banking is defined as accepting, for the purpose of lending or investment, of deposits of money from the public, repayable on demand or otherwise, and withdraw able by cheque, draft, order or otherwise "Banking Company" means any company which transacts the business of banking in India. Company means any company as defined in Section 3 of the Companies Act, 1956 and includes a foreign company within the meaning of Section 591 of that Act.

Understanding the role of (Organised Sector) Banks and (unorganised Sector) Money Lenders.

Organised Sector: Organised sector consist of the banking system comprises of scheduled & non-scheduled banks.

In India, banks have been broadly classified into scheduled and non-scheduled banks. A Scheduled Bank is that which has been included in the Second Schedule of the Reserve Bank of India Act, 1934 and fulfills the two conditions:  It has paid-up capital and reserves of at least Rs. 5 lakhs. It ensures to the Reserve Bank that its operations are not detrimental to the interest of the depositors; It is a corporation or a cooperative society and not a partnership or a single owner firm.

The banks which are not included in the Second Schedule of the Reserve Bank of India Act are non-scheduled banks.

Scheduled Banks consists of Scheduled Commercial Banks which are:

Public Sector Banks Private Sector Banks Regional Rural Banks Foreign Banks

Scheduled Co-operative Banks consist of Urban Co-operative Banks and Rural Cooperative Banks.

Non-Scheduled Banks: Non-scheduled banks also function in the Indian banking space, in the form of Local Area Banks (LAB). Local area banks are banks that are set up under the scheme announced by the government of India in 1996, for the establishment of new private banks of a local nature; with jurisdiction over a maximum of three contiguous districts. LABs aid in the mobilisation of funds of rural and semi urban districts.

Payment Banks: On 19 August 2015, the Reserve Bank of India gave "in-principle" licences to eleven entities to launch payments banks:

Aditya Birla Nuvo

Airtel M Commerce Services Cholamandalam Distribution Services Department of Posts

FINO PayTech

National Securities Depository Reliance Industries

Dilip Shanghvi, Sun Pharmaceuticals Vijay Shekhar Sharma, Paytm

Tech Mahindra Vodafone M-Pesa

The "in-principle" license is valid for 18 months within which the entities must fulfill the requirements. They are not allowed to engage in banking activities within the period. The RBI will consider grant full licenses under Section 22 of the Banking Regulation Act, 1949, after it is satisfied that the conditions have been fulfilled.

Small Finance Banks: Small finance banks are a type of niche banks in India. Banks with a small finance bank license can provide basic banking service of acceptance of deposits and lending. The aim behind these to provide financial inclusion sections of the economy not being served by other banks, such as small business units, small and marginal farmers, micro and small industries and unorganised sector entities

On Sept 16, 2015, The Reserve Bank of India (RBI) has decided to grant "inprinciple" approval to the following 10 applicants to set up small finance banks under the "Guidelines for Licensing of Small Finance Banks in the private sector" (Guidelines) issued on November 27, 2014.

Names of selected applicants

Au Financiers (India) Ltd., Jaipur Capital Local Area Bank Ltd., Jalandhar Disha Microfin Private Ltd., Ahmedabad Equitas Holdings P Limited, Chennai

ESAF Microfinance and Investments Private Ltd., Chennai Janalakshmi Financial Services Private Limited, Bengaluru

Indigenous Bankers (IBs): Indigenous bankers are individuals or private firms who receive deposits and give loans and thereby operate as banks. IBs accept deposits as well as lend money. Further their lending operations are completely unsupervised and unregulated. Over the years, the significance of IBs has declined due to growing organised banking sector.

Money Lenders (MLs): They are those whose primary business is money lending. Money lending in India is very popular both in urban and rural areas. Interest rates are generally high. Large amount of loans are given for unproductive purposes. The operations of money lenders are prompt, informal and flexible. The borrowers are mostly poor farmers, artisans, petty traders and manual workers. Over the years the role of money lenders has declined due to the growing importance of organised banking sector.

Non - Banking Financial Companies (NBFCs): NBFC stands for non banking financial company that was created by the government of India under the Company Act 1956 to provide access to poor sections of the society to banking facilities. Though NBFC performs many of the functions of a bank, there are many differences. NBFC cannot accept money deposits in the manner of banks NBFC cannot issue checks drawn on itself Normally, a NBFC is engaged in the business of loans and advances, acquisition of shares, debentures, stocks, bonds and securities issued by the government. It also indulges in hire- purchase, leasing, insurance and chit business. They consist of:

Chit Funds: Chit funds are savings institutions. It has regular members who make periodic subscriptions to the fund. The beneficiary may be selected by drawing of lots. Chit fund is more popular in Kerala and Tamil Nadu. RBI has no control over the lending activities of chit funds.

Nidhis: Nidhis operate as a kind of mutual benefit for their members only. The loans are given to members at a reasonable rate of interest. Nidhis operate particularly in South India.

Loan Or Finance Companies: Loan companies are found in all parts of the country. Their total capital consists of borrowings, deposits and owned funds. They give loans to retailers, wholesalers, artisans and self-employed persons. They offer a high rate of interest along with other incentives to attract deposits. They charge high rate of interest varying from 36% to 48% p.a.

Finance Brokers: They are found in all major urban markets specially in cloth, grain and commodity markets. They act as middlemen between lenders and borrowers. They charge commission for their services.


The Importance of Banking

Banking is an essential component of modern economies and serves as the backbone of financial systems across the globe. It encompasses a broad spectrum of services, ranging from deposit-taking to lending, investment management, and payment processing. The role of banks in facilitating economic development and ensuring financial stability cannot be overstated. The following discusses the key reasons why banking is important both on an individual and societal level.

Facilitates Economic Growth and Development

Banks play a critical role in fostering economic growth by mobilizing savings and allocating capital efficiently. Through the process of deposit-taking, banks collect funds from individuals, businesses, and institutions. These funds are then used to provide loans for various productive activities such as business expansion, infrastructure development, and consumer spending. By channeling savings into investments, banks help stimulate economic activity and create jobs.

Moreover, banks support innovation by providing financing for research and development (R&D), technology adoption, and entrepreneurship. For example, venture capital firms, which are often backed by banks, invest in startups that have the potential to disrupt industries. In this way, banks indirectly fuel technological advancements, helping economies become more competitive in a globalized world.

Promotes Financial Inclusion: Banking institutions are central to achieving financial inclusion, which is the accessibility of affordable financial services to all segments of society, including low-income groups and marginalized communities.

banking, banks empower individuals who previously lacked access to formal financial systems. This inclusivity is crucial because it gives people the tools to manage their money, build wealth, and safeguard against financial risks.

For example, microfinance institutions (MFIs), often affiliated with larger banks, provide small loans to entrepreneurs in developing countries who do not have access to traditional credit markets. By helping small business owners expand their operations, banks can alleviate poverty and drive socio-economic mobility. Financial inclusion also reduces reliance on informal lending sources, which tend to have exploitative interest rates and terms.

Provides a Secure Medium for Savings and Investments

The security of deposits is one of the most significant functions of the banking system. Banks offer individuals and businesses a safe place to store their money, providing protection against theft, fraud, or loss due to unforeseen circumstances. In most countries, government- backed deposit insurance schemes (such as the FDIC in the United States) guarantee the safety of deposits up to a certain limit, further enhancing consumer confidence in the banking system.

Additionally, banks provide investment products like bonds, mutual funds, and retirement accounts, which help individuals build long-term wealth. For businesses, banks offer services such as treasury management, risk hedging, and trade financing, all of which contribute to greater financial security and growth opportunities. As a result, banks not only safeguard people's savings but also enable them to make informed decisions about how to invest and grow their wealth.

Enables Efficient Payment Systems

The ability to facilitate efficient, safe, and timely payments is another important function of banks. Banks provide various payment services, including wire transfers, online banking, and card payments, making it possible for individuals and businesses to exchange money quickly and securely. The advent of digital banking and mobile payments has revolutionized how people transfer money, pay bills, and make purchases, increasing convenience and reducing transaction costs.

For businesses, the payment systems offered by banks are vital for conducting daily operations, such as paying suppliers, managing payroll, and receiving customer payments. Banks also support the international trade ecosystem by providing foreign exchange services and letters of credit, which are essential for facilitating cross-border transactions. In this way, the banking sector helps create a seamless flow of goods, services, and capital both locally and globally.

Risk Management and Financial Stability

Banks help manage financial risks through various mechanisms such as lending diversification, risk assessment, and the implementation of safeguards like capital reserves. By evaluating the creditworthiness of borrowers, banks reduce the chances of bad loans and defaults. Additionally, banks use sophisticated financial products like insurance and derivatives to hedge against potential risks such as interest rate fluctuations or currency exchange rate volatility.

Moreover, a stable banking system is essential for overall economic stability. Central banks, such as the Federal Reserve in the U.S. or the European Central Bank, oversee and regulate commercial banks to ensure the safety of the financial system and the wider economy. During times of financial crises, central banks can step in to provide liquidity and prevent the collapse of banks, as seen during the global financial crisis of 2007-2008. In this way, banking not only manages individual risks but also supports systemic stability.

Supports Government and Public Sector Financing

Governments rely heavily on banks for the financing of public sector projects, budget deficits, and national development plans. Through mechanisms like government bonds and Treasury bills, banks assist governments in raising the capital necessary for building infrastructure, funding social programs, and addressing public debt. Moreover, the banking sector plays a critical role in monetary policy implementation by working with central banks to influence interest rates and money supply.

For example, when a central bank wants to stimulate the economy, it may lower interest rates to encourage borrowing. Banks, as intermediaries, facilitate this process by adjusting their own lending rates in line with the central bank's policy. This relationship ensures that the broader economy can respond to changes in government fiscal and monetary strategies, which are crucial for maintaining stable economic growth.

**Encourages Financial Discipline and Literacy**

Banks also contribute to improving financial literacy by offering educational resources, tools, and advisory services. Many banks provide online platforms that allow individuals to track their spending, set budgets, and plan for future expenses. These services help customers develop better financial habits, make informed decisions, and avoid financial pitfalls. Financial discipline, such as saving for emergencies, paying off debts, and investing for the future, can significantly improve an individual's financial well-being. By offering products like fixed deposits, retirement accounts, and automatic savings plans.

History of Banking in India

The history of banking in India spans several millennia, reflecting the country's diverse economic, cultural, and political landscape. From ancient times, where trade and commerce were conducted using barter systems and coins, to the establishment of modern banking institutions, the evolution of banking in India has been a crucial factor in shaping the country's economy. Below is an overview of the key milestones in the development of banking in India.

Early Banking Practices in India (Ancient and Medieval Period)

In ancient India, banking was not formalized in the way we understand it today, but there were various institutions that provided financial services. The concept of moneylending can be traced back to the Vedic period (around 1500 BCE to 500 BCE). Ancient texts, such as the Arthashastra written by Kautilya (Chanakya), mention the roles of shroffs (moneylenders) and bankers, who helped in the exchange of money and commodities. Traders also engaged in lending and borrowing practices, though these were informal and often community-based.

During the medieval period, Indian banking saw the rise of moneylenders and Hundi (a type of promissory note). Wealthy traders and financiers used Hundis for remittances and credit. The structure of the Indian banking system in this era was deeply intertwined with the merchant class, with bankers often providing credit for trade and commerce.

The Colonial Era (1770s–1947)

The foundation of modern banking in India was laid during British rule. The first formal banking institutions were established by the British to cater to the needs of the colonial economy. Key events in the development of Indian banking during this period include:

The Establishment of the Bank of Calcutta (1806): The Bank of Calcutta, later renamed the Bank of Bengal, was the first joint-stock bank in India. It was established to cater to the needs of British traders and the East India Company. This marked the beginning of the formal banking system in India.

The Formation of the Presidency Banks: Following the establishment of the Bank of Bengal, two more presidency banks were created: the Bank of Bombay (1840) and the Bank of Madras (1843). These banks were established in the presidencies of British India and played a central role in financing colonial trade and facilitating the collection of taxes. The Reserve Bank of India (RBI): In 1935, the Reserve Bank of India (RBI) was established as the central bank of India. Initially, RBI was set up to regulate currency and manage the monetary system, but over time.

banking sector and formulating policies to promote economic growth.

The Emergence of Commercial Banks: With the rise of industrialization in India, several private commercial banks were established, such as the Punjab National Bank (1894), Allahabad Bank (1865), and Indian Bank (1907). These banks catered to the growing needs of businesses and the emerging middle class.

Post-Independence Banking Reforms (1947–1970)

After India gained independence in 1947, the banking system underwent several significant reforms. The Indian government recognized the need to channel banking resources into sectors that would promote economic development, particularly agriculture, industry, and infrastructure. Key milestones include:

Nationalization of Banks (1969): One of the most significant events in the history of Indian banking was the nationalization of 14 major commercial banks by then-Prime Minister Indira Gandhi in 1969. This was done with the aim of aligning the banking sector with the socio-economic goals of the newly independent nation. The government sought to make banking services more accessible to rural areas, ensuring that credit would be available to underdeveloped and agricultural sectors. The nationalization of banks also aimed at controlling the concentration of economic power in the hands of a few private entities.

Establishment of Regional Rural Banks (RRBs) (1975): In 1975, the Indian government created Regional Rural Banks to improve access to credit in rural and remote areas. These banks were aimed at providing financial services to the underserved rural population, particularly farmers, small entrepreneurs, and artisans.

Introduction of the Lead Bank Scheme (1969): Under this scheme, the government designated certain banks as "lead banks" for specific districts, with the responsibility of developing the rural economy in those areas. The goal was to ensure the flow of credit to backward and rural regions, promoting inclusive growth.

Liberalization and Privatization (1990s)

The 1990s marked a period of economic liberalization in India, and with it, came a wave of banking reforms. The Indian government undertook measures to modernize the banking system and make it more competitive in the globalized economy. Key reforms during this period include:Economic Liberalization (1991): The economic reforms initiated in 1991, under Prime Minister Narasimha Rao and Finance Minister Manmohan Singh, significantly impacted the banking.

New Private Sector Banks: Following the liberalization, private sector banks were allowed to enter the Indian market, creating increased competition in the banking sector. Banks like HDFC Bank (1994), ICICI Bank (1994), Axis Bank (1994), and Kotak Mahindra Bank (2003) became major players in the industry. These banks introduced innovative products and services, and they were among the first to embrace technology, including ATM networks, electronic banking, and online banking.

Reforms by the RBI: The Reserve Bank of India took several steps to strengthen the banking sector, including measures to enhance the capital adequacy ratio, improve asset quality, and encourage the adoption of technology. The introduction of the Asset Reconstruction Companies (ARCs) in the early 2000s helped address non-performing assets (NPAs) in the banking system.

Modern Banking (2000s–Present)

In the 21st century, Indian banking has undergone major transformations, driven by technological advancements, financial inclusion initiatives, and the growing role of private and foreign banks.

Technological Advancements: The introduction of digital banking, mobile banking, and online payment systems has revolutionized the way banking services are delivered. The India Stack, a collection of application programming interfaces (APIs), has facilitated digital payments, eKYC (electronic Know Your Customer), and biometric- based authentication through Aadhaar (India's biometric identity system).

Pradhan Mantri Jan Dhan Yojana (PMJDY): Launched in 2014, the PMJDY aimed at promoting financial inclusion by providing access to basic banking services for all citizens, especially those in rural and underserved areas. The program led to the opening of millions of new bank accounts and encouraged savings among India's low-income populations.

Mergers and Consolidation: The Indian government has undertaken a series of mergers of public sector banks to create larger, more competitive institutions. In 2020, the government announced the merger of 10 public sector banks into four entities, aiming to strengthen the sector and improve financial stability.

Financial Technology (FinTech): The rise of fintech companies in India has created new avenues for financial services delivery, including digital lending, mobile wallets, peer-to-peer lending, and block chain-based solutions.

Types of Bank Accounts

Bank accounts are essential financial tools that allow individuals and businesses to store, manage, and access their money securely. Banks offer various types of accounts to cater to the different needs of their customers, ranging from basic savings accounts to specialized business accounts. Here are the main types of bank accounts that customers can open in India (and many other countries) to fulfill different financial objectives:

Savings Account

A savings account is one of the most common and basic types of bank accounts. It is primarily used by individuals to save money while earning a small amount of interest on their balance. Savings accounts are designed to be low- risk, easily accessible, and a safe place to store money for short- to medium- term savings.

Key Features:

Interest: Savings accounts earn interest on the deposited amount. The interest rate varies from bank to bank but is typically lower than other types of investment accounts.

Liquidity: Funds can be withdrawn easily at any time, making this account highly liquid.

Minimum Balance Requirement: Some savings accounts require a minimum balance to be maintained.

Accessibility: Account holders can access their funds through ATMs, online banking, and branch visits.

Types of Savings Accounts:

Basic Savings Bank Deposit Account (BSBDA): A government initiative to promote financial inclusion, this account is available with no minimum balance requirement and offers basic banking services.

Senior Citizens' Savings Account: This type of account is specifically designed for senior citizens and typically offers higher interest rates.

Women's Savings Account: Some banks offer savings accounts with added benefits like higher interest rates or zero balance requirements for women.

Current Account

A current account is primarily used by businesses, organizations, and individuals who need frequent access to their funds for day-to-day transactions. Unlike savings accounts, current accounts do not offer interest on the deposited amount.

Key Features:

No Interest: Current accounts usually do not earn interest.

High Transaction Limit: Current accounts allow for a higher volume of transactions than savings accounts.

Overdraft Facility: Many banks offer an overdraft facility, allowing customers to withdraw more than their current balance up to an agreed limit.

Frequent Transactions: Suitable for individuals or businesses that need to make frequent payments or deposits, such as paying suppliers or receiving payments from customers.

Types of Current Accounts:

Standard Current Account: The most common type for businesses and professionals. This account is used for managing large numbers of daily transactions.

Business Current Account: Tailored for business use, this account offers additional features like bulk payment processing, trade finance services, and integration with accounting software.

Fixed Deposit Account (FD)

A fixed deposit (FD) is a type of investment account where the account holder deposits a lump sum amount of money for a fixed tenure at a predetermined interest rate. The amount cannot be withdrawn before the maturity date without incurring a penalty.

Key Features:

Fixed Interest: FDs earn a higher rate of interest compared to savings accounts.

Tenure: The tenure of a fixed deposit can range from a few weeks to several years.

Liquidity: Funds in a fixed deposit are locked in for the duration of the term, though premature withdrawals are allowed with penalties.

Guaranteed Returns: Fixed deposits are low-risk and offer guaranteed returns, making them a popular choice for conservative investors.

Types of Fixed Deposits:

Tax-Saving Fixed Deposit: This type of FD is eligible for tax benefits under Section 80C of the Income Tax Act, but it has a lock-in period of 5 years.

Senior Citizens' Fixed Deposit: Senior citizens often receive higher interest rates on their FDs.

Cumulative and Non-Cumulative Fixed Deposit: In cumulative FDs, the interest earned is reinvested, while in non-cumulative FDs, interest is paid out periodically (monthly, quarterly, or annually).

Recurring Deposit Account (RD)

A recurring deposit (RD) account is an account where a fixed amount of money is deposited every month for a specific period. RDs are suitable for individuals who want to build savings over time by making regular deposits.

Key Features:

Regular Deposits: The customer agrees to deposit a fixed amount every month.

Interest Rate: The interest rate on an RD is usually higher than a savings account, but lower than a fixed deposit.

Tenure: The tenure can range from 6 months to 10 years, with the principal amount being locked in for the chosen period.

Liquidity: Funds cannot be withdrawn easily before the maturity date, but loans against RDs are possible in some cases.

Types of Recurring Deposit Accounts:

Regular RD: The most common recurring deposit account, where the customer deposits a fixed amount monthly for a predetermined tenure.

Senior Citizens' RD: Some banks offer higher interest rates on recurring deposits for senior citizens.

Demat Account

A demat account (short for "dematerialized account") is used for holding shares, bonds, and other securities in electronic form. It is mandatory for individuals wishing to trade in stocks or other securities through the stock exchanges.

Key Features: Holding Securities Electronically: Securities such as stocks and bonds are stored electronically in a demat account, eliminating the need for physical certificates.

Trading: Investors can buy, sell, or transfer securities through a demat account.

Charges: Demat accounts may come with account maintenance fees, transaction fees, or annual charges.

NRI Accounts (Non-Resident Indian Accounts) Non-Resident Indians (NRIs) who live abroad can open special types of bank accounts to manage their finances in India. These accounts include:

NRE (Non-Resident External) Account: An account where NRIs can deposit income earned outside India. The balance is held in Indian rupees, and the interest earned is tax-

NRO (Non-Resident Ordinary) Account: Used to manage income earned in India (e.g., rent, dividends). The interest earned on NRO accounts is subject to tax in India.

FCNR (Foreign Currency Non-Resident) Account: A type of fixed deposit account in which the deposit is held in foreign currency (e.g., USD, GBP), and the interest is exempt from Indian income tax.

Current Accounts for Foreign Exchange

For businesses or individuals engaged in international trade or transactions involving foreign currency, banks offer specialized current accounts for foreign exchange. These accounts facilitate the transfer of foreign currency and make it easier to deal with international transactions.

Joint Accounts

A joint account is an account held by two or more individuals who have equal rights over the account. Joint accounts can be opened in various types, including savings, current, or fixed deposit accounts. There are different types of joint accounts, such as:

Joint Account with Both Parties' Signature: Both account holders must sign to authorize any transaction.

Either or Survivor Account: Either one of the account holders can operate the account, and the survivor can continue using it in case of the death of the other account holder.

Banker and Customer Relationship Meaning

The banker-customer relationship refers to the legal and contractual relationship between a bank (the banker) and its customer. This relationship is governed by various laws, regulations, and contractual agreements, and it encompasses a range of rights, obligations, and responsibilities for both parties. Here's a breakdown of the key aspects of the banker- customer relationship:

Deposit and Withdrawal Services: One of the primary functions of a bank is to provide deposit and withdrawal services to its customers. Customers deposit funds into their accounts for safekeeping and may withdraw these funds as needed. The bank is obligated to keep the deposited funds safe and accessible to the customer upon request.

Payments and Transactions: Banks facilitate various payment and transaction services for their customers, including transfers, bill payments, and clearing of checks. Customers rely on banks to process these transactions accurately and efficiently, while banks are responsible for ensuring the security and integrity of the payment systems.

Credit and Lending Services: Banks extend credit and lending facilities to customers in the form of loans, mortgages, overdrafts, and other credit products. Customers borrow funds from the bank for various purposes, and the bank assesses the creditworthiness of the customer and manages the associated risks.

Fiduciary Duties: Banks owe fiduciary duties to their customers, including duties of care, confidentiality, and loyalty. Banks are expected to act in the best interests of their customers, maintain confidentiality of customer information, and avoid conflicts of interest.

Regulatory Compliance: Banks are subject to extensive regulation and supervision by banking authorities to ensure the safety, soundness, and stability of the banking system. Banks must comply with regulatory requirements related to capital adequacy, risk management, anti-money laundering, customer protection, and other areas.

Contractual Agreements: The banker-customer relationship is governed by contractual agreements, such as account opening documents, loan agreements, and terms and conditions for banking services. These contracts define the rights and obligations of both parties and provide a legal framework for the relationship.

Dispute Resolution: In the event of disputes or disagreements between the bank and its customer, mechanisms for dispute resolution, such as arbitration or mediation, may be available to resolve issues in a fair and impartial manner.

Overall, the banker-customer relationship is based on trust, mutual obligations, and legal rights, and it is essential for the smooth functioning of the banking system and the provision of financial services to individuals, businesses, and other entities.

Meaning of Banker and Customer

The terms "banking" and "customer" are fundamental concepts in the financial industry, particularly in the context of banking services and relationships. Here's a breakdown of each term:

Banking:

Definition: Banking refers to the business activity of providing financial services such as accepting deposits, lending money, and facilitating transactions. Banks, credit unions, and other financial institutions are primary providers of banking services.

Functions: Banking encompasses a range of functions and activities, including:

Depository Services: Banks accept deposits from individuals, businesses, and other entities, providing a safe place to store funds.

Lending: Banks extend credit to borrowers in the form of loans, mortgages, lines of credit, and other financing products.

Payment Services: Banks facilitate the transfer of funds between individuals, businesses, and institutions through various payment methods such as checks, electronic transfers, and debit/credit cards.

Investment Services: Some banks offer investment products and services, including wealth management, brokerage services, and retirement planning.

Risk Management: Banks engage in risk management activities to assess and mitigate various types of risk, including credit risk, market risk, operational risk, and compliance risk.

Regulation: Banking is subject to extensive regulation and oversight by governmental authorities to ensure the safety and soundness of the financial system, protect consumers, and maintain financial stability.

Customer:

Definition: A customer, in the context of banking, refers to an individual, business, or organization that uses the services of a bank or financial institution. Customers engage with banks to conduct financial transactions, manage their funds, and access various banking products and services.

Types of Customers: Customers of banks can include:

Retail Customers: Individuals who use banking services for personal financial needs, such as checking accounts, savings accounts, loans, and mortgages.

Commercial Customers: Businesses and corporations that use banking services for managing cash flow, making payments, obtaining financing, and other financial activities.

Institutional Customers: Financial institutions, government agencies, non-profit organizations, and other entities that require specialized banking services, such as custody services, clearing and settlement, and treasury management.

Relationship Management: Banks typically assign relationship managers or account managers to oversee customer relationships, provide personalized service, and address customer needs and inquiries.

Legal Rights and Responsibilities: Customers have certain legal rights and responsibilities when engaging with banks, including the right to access account information, the obligation to provide accurate information, and protections against unfair or deceptive practices.

In summary, banking refers to the business of providing financial services, while a customer is an individual or entity that uses those services. The relationship between banks and customers is built on trust, transparency, and the mutual fulfillment of financial needs and objectives.

Permitted Activities of Commercial Banks in India

Commercial banks in India are regulated by the Reserve Bank of India (RBI) and are authorized to undertake a wide range of banking activities. These activities are outlined in the Banking Regulation Act, 1949, and subsequent regulations and guidelines issued by the RBI. Here are the permitted activities of commercial banks in India:

Accepting Deposits:

Commercial banks can accept various types of deposits from individuals, businesses, and other entities. These include savings accounts, current accounts, fixed deposits, recurring deposits, and specialized deposit schemes.

Granting Loans and Advances:

Commercial banks are authorized to extend credit to borrowers in the form of loans, overdrafts, lines of credit, and other financing products. This includes loans for various purposes such as personal loans, home loans, auto loans, business loans, and agricultural loans.

Providing Payment Services:

Banks facilitate the transfer of funds between individuals, businesses, and institutions through various payment services. These include check clearing, electronic funds transfer (NEFT, RTGS, IMPS), mobile banking, internet banking, and debit/credit card services.

Issuing of Debit and Credit Cards:

Commercial banks issue debit cards and credit cards to their customers, allowing them to make purchases, withdraw cash, and access other banking services.

Foreign Exchange Services:

Banks are permitted to provide foreign exchange services, including buying and selling foreign currency, remittance services, issuing traveler's checks, and offering foreign currency accounts.

Investment Services:

Commercial banks can offer investment products and services to their customers, including mutual funds, insurance products, pension plans, and wealth management services.

Treasury Operations:

Banks engage in treasury operations to manage their own funds and investments. This includes trading in money market instruments, government securities, corporate bonds, and other financial instruments.

Advisory Services:

Banks may offer financial advisory services to their customers, including investment advice, financial planning, risk management, and other consultancy services.

Safe Deposit Lockers:

Banks provide safe deposit locker facilities to customers for the safekeeping of valuable documents, jewelry, and other items.

Agency Services:

Commercial banks can act as agents for their customers in various financial transactions, such as collecting and remitting funds, issuing demand drafts, and executing standing instructions.

These are some of the primary activities permitted for commercial banks in India. However, banks are also subject to regulatory restrictions and guidelines issued by the RBI to ensure the safety and soundness of the banking system and to protect the interests of depositors and customers.

General & Special features of relationship between banker and customer

The relationship between a banker and a customer is characterized by several general and special features, which define the nature of their interactions and responsibilities. Here's a breakdown of these features:

General Features:

Contractual Basis: The relationship between a banker and a customer is founded on contractual agreements, which outline the terms and conditions governing the provision of banking services. These contracts may include account opening documents, loan agreements, and terms of service for various banking products.

Fiduciary Duty: Banks owe a fiduciary duty to their customers, which entails a high standard of care, loyalty, and confidentiality. Banks are expected to act in the best interests of their customers, maintain the confidentiality of customer information, and avoid conflicts of interest.

Financial Intermediation: Banks serve as financial intermediaries between savers and borrowers, facilitating the allocation of funds from surplus units (depositors) to deficit units (borrowers). Customers entrust their funds to banks for safekeeping and may also seek credit or lending services from banks.

Regulatory Compliance: Banks are subject to extensive regulation and supervision by banking authorities to ensure the safety, soundness, and stability of the banking system. Compliance with regulatory requirements is essential to protect the interests of customers and maintain the integrity of the banking system.

Principle of Good Faith: The relationship between a banker and a customer is based on the principle of good faith, requiring both parties to act honestly, fairly, and transparently in their dealings with each other. This principle underpins the trust and confidence essential to the functioning of the banking relationship.


Special Features:


Confidentiality: Banks are required to maintain the confidentiality of customer information and financial transactions. Special laws and regulations govern the disclosure of customer data, ensuring that sensitive information is protected from unauthorized access or disclosure.

Deposit Insurance: Many jurisdictions provide deposit insurance schemes to protect customer deposits in the event of a bank failure. Deposit insurance helps to enhance confidence in the banking system and reassure customers that their funds are safe.

Payment Systems: Banks play a central role in payment systems, providing services for the transfer of funds, clearing of checks, and settlement of transactions. The efficiency and reliability of payment systems are critical to the smooth functioning of the economy.

Credit Facilities: Banks offer various credit facilities to customers, including loans, mortgages, overdrafts, and credit cards. These credit facilities enable customers to access funds for personal or business purposes, subject to credit assessment and risk management by the bank.

Investment Services: Banks may provide investment services to customers, such as wealth management, brokerage, and advisory services. These services help customers manage their investments and achieve their financial goals, often in conjunction with other banking products and services.

Overall, the relationship between a banker and a customer is characterized by trust, professionalism, and regulatory oversight, with both parties having rights, obligations, and responsibilities that are governed by contractual agreements, legal principles, and industry standards.

Rights and Duties of Banker and Customer

The relationship between a banker and a customer is defined by specific rights and duties for both parties, which are outlined in contractual agreements, regulatory requirements, and legal principles. Here's a breakdown of the rights and duties of each:

Rights of the Banker:

Right to Payment of Debts: The bank has the right to receive payment of debts owed to it by the customer, including loan repayments, fees, and charges for banking services.

Right to Setoff: In certain circumstances, the bank may have the right to set off any debts owed by the customer against funds held in the customer's accounts with the bank.

Right to Charge Interest and Fees: Banks have the right to charge interest on loans and credit facilities provided to customers, as well as fees for banking services and transactions.

Right to Refuse Services: Banks may have the right to refuse to provide certain services or products to customers, especially if the customer does not meet the bank's eligibility criteria or if there are concerns about legal or regulatory compliance.

Right to Terminate the Relationship: Banks have the right to terminate the banking relationship with a customer in accordance with the terms of the contractual agreement or for reasons such as non-payment of debts, fraudulent activities, or breaches of banking regulations.

Duties of the Banker:

Duty of Care: Banks owe a duty of care to their customers, which includes exercising reasonable skill, care, and diligence in providing banking services, managing customer accounts, and safeguarding customer funds.

Confidentiality Duty: Banks have a duty to maintain the confidentiality of customer information and financial transactions, except where disclosure is required by law or authorized by the customer.

Duty to Provide Information: Banks must provide customers with clear and accurate information about the terms and conditions of banking products and services, including fees, charges, interest rates, and risks.

Duty to Protect Customer Funds: Banks are responsible for safeguarding customer funds held in accounts with the bank, including taking measures to prevent fraud, theft, or unauthorized access to customer accounts.

Duty to Comply with Regulations: Banks are obligated to comply with applicable banking laws, regulations, and industry standards, including requirements related to anti-money laundering, consumer protection, data privacy, and financial stability.

Rights of the Customer:

Right to Access Funds: Customers have the right to access funds held in their accounts with the bank and to withdraw or transfer funds as needed, subject to the terms and conditions of the account agreement.

Right to Privacy: Customers have the right to privacy and confidentiality of their personal and financial information, and banks must obtain consent before disclosing customer information to third parties, except as required by law.

Right to Receive Information: Customers have the right to receive clear and accurate information about banking products and services, including fees, charges, interest rates, and terms and conditions.

Right to Redress: Customers have the right to seek redress or resolution of disputes with the bank, including complaints about account services, fees, charges, or other banking practices.

Right to Fair Treatment: Customers have the right to fair and equitable treatment by the bank, including timely and courteous service, transparent disclosure of terms and conditions, and protection from unfair or deceptive practices.

Duties of the Customer:

Duty to Provide Information: Customers have a duty to provide accurate and complete information to the bank when opening accounts, applying for credit, or conducting financial transactions, including information required for identity verification and compliance with anti-money laundering regulations.

Duty to Pay Debts: Customers are obligated to repay any debts owed to the bank, including loans, overdrafts, and credit card balances, according to the terms and conditions of the contractual agreement.

Duty to Notify of Errors or Disputes: Customers have a duty to promptly notify the bank of any errors, discrepancies, or unauthorized transactions in their accounts and to cooperate with the bank in resolving disputes or investigating fraudulent activities.

Duty to Comply with Terms and Conditions: Customers are required to comply with the terms and conditions of their account agreements, loan contracts, and other banking arrangements, including restrictions on account usage, minimum balance requirements, and payment deadlines.

Duty to Protect Account Information: Customers have a duty to take reasonable measures to protect their account information, passwords, and security credentials from unauthorized access or disclosure, including safeguarding ATM cards, PINs, and online banking credentials.

Overall, the rights and duties of both the banker and the customer are intended to promote a fair, transparent, and mutually beneficial banking relationship, while also ensuring compliance with legal and regulatory requirements and protecting the interests of both parties.

## CHAPTER 2

## DEPOSIT ACCOUNTS

Deposit accounts are a type of bank account that allows customers to deposit money with a financial institution for safekeeping and to earn interest on their deposits. These accounts are commonly used for everyday banking transactions, such as receiving payments, making withdrawals, and managing personal finances. Here are the key features and types of deposit accounts:

Key Features:

Deposit and Withdrawal: Deposit accounts allow customers to deposit funds into the account, either in person, through electronic transfers, or by depositing checks. Customers can also withdraw funds from the account as needed, typically through electronic transfers, ATM withdrawals, checks, or in-person withdrawals at a bank branch.

Interest Earnings: Many deposit accounts earn interest on the funds deposited, although the interest rates vary depending on the type of account and prevailing market conditions. The interest is usually calculated on the account balance and credited to the account periodically, such as monthly or quarterly.

Safety and Security: Deposit accounts are considered safe and secure because they are typically insured by government deposit insurance schemes, such as the Federal Deposit Insurance Corporation (FDIC) in the United States. Deposit insurance protects customers' funds up to a certain limit in the event of bank failure.

Accessibility: Deposit accounts offer customers easy access to their funds, allowing them to make transactions and manage their money conveniently. Many banks offer online banking services, mobile banking apps, and ATM networks to provide customers with 24/7 access to their accounts.

Regulatory Compliance: Deposit accounts are subject to banking regulations and oversight by government authorities to ensure the safety, soundness, and integrity of the banking system. Banks must comply with regulations related to account opening, customer identification, anti-money laundering, and consumer protection.

Types of Deposit Accounts:

Savings Accounts: Savings accounts are designed for customers to save money over time while earning interest on their deposits. These accounts typically have no or minimal transaction fees and may have restrictions on the number of withdrawals allowed per month.

Checking Accounts: Checking accounts are used for everyday banking transactions, such as writing checks, making electronic payments, and using debit cards. These accounts may or may not earn interest, and they often have higher transaction limits compared to savings accounts.

Money Market Accounts: Money market accounts combine features of both savings and checking accounts, offering higher interest rates than regular savings accounts while still providing check-writing and debit card access. These accounts may require a higher minimum balance to open and maintain.

Certificates of Deposit (CDs): CDs are time deposit accounts that require customers to deposit funds for a fixed period, ranging from a few months to several years, in exchange for a higher interest rate. Early withdrawal of funds from a CD may result in penalties.

Individual Retirement Accounts (IRAs): IRAs are tax-advantaged retirement savings accounts that allow individuals to save for retirement while potentially reducing their tax liability. These accounts can hold a variety of investments, including stocks, bonds, mutual funds, and CDs.

Business Deposit Accounts: Banks offer deposit accounts tailored to the needs of businesses, including business savings accounts, business checking accounts, and merchant services accounts for processing payments.

Overall, deposit accounts are essential financial tools that provide individuals and businesses with a secure and convenient way to manage their money, save for the future, and achieve their financial goals.

requirements as per the guidelines issued by the Reserve Bank of India (RBI) and individual bank policies. Here's a general overview of the processes:

Opening Operations:

Fixed Deposit Account:

Documentation: The customer needs to provide identity proof, address proof, and other KYC (Know Your Customer) documents as per the bank's requirements.

Deposit Amount: The customer decides the deposit amount and tenor of the fixed deposit.

Interest Rate: The bank informs the customer about the prevailing interest rates for the chosen deposit term.

Account Opening Form: The customer fills out the fixed deposit account opening form, specifying details such as deposit amount, deposit term, and nominee details.

Deposit: The customer deposits the required amount with the bank.

Fixed Deposit Receipt: The bank issues a fixed deposit receipt containing details of the deposit, such as deposit amount, term, maturity date, and interest rate.

Recurring Deposit Account:

Documentation: Similar to fixed deposits, the customer provides necessary documents for KYC compliance.

Deposit Amount: The customer decides the monthly deposit amount.

Interest Rate: The bank informs the customer about the applicable interest rate for recurring deposits.

Account Opening Form: The customer fills out the recurring deposit account opening form, specifying the deposit amount, deposit term, and other relevant details.

Initial Deposit: The customer makes the initial deposit required to open  .

Savings Account:

Documentation: Customers provide identity proof, address proof, and other KYC documents as required.

Account Opening Form: The customer fills out the savings account opening form, providing personal details and signature.

Initial Deposit: The customer deposits the minimum initial deposit required to open a savings account.

Account Activation: The bank verifies the provided documents and activates the savings account.

Passbook/Statement: The bank issues a passbook or provides access to online banking facilities for the customer to monitor account transactions.

Current Account:

Documentation: Similar to savings accounts, customers provide KYC documents.

Account Opening Form: The customer fills out the current account opening form, providing business details, proprietor/partnership details, and authorized signatories.

Initial Deposit: The customer deposits the minimum initial deposit required to open a current account.

Account Activation: The bank verifies the provided documents and activates the current account.

Checkbook and Other Services: The bank provides a checkbook, along with other services such as internet banking and overdraft facilities, as per the account type and customer requirements.

Closure Operations:

Fixed Deposit Account, Recurring Deposit Account, Savings Account, and Current Account:

Account Closure Request: The account holder submits a written request for closure of the account.

Clearance of Dues: The account holder settles any outstanding dues or charges on the account.

Return of Documents: The account holder returns any unused checkbooks, debit cards, or other bank-issued documents.

Closure Form: The account holder fills out an account closure form provided by the bank.

Balance Transfer: For savings and current accounts, any remaining balance is transferred to the account holder's specified account or provided in the form of a demand draft.

Closure Confirmation: The bank issues a closure confirmation letter or statement once the account closure process is completed.

It's important to note that specific procedures and documentation requirements may vary slightly between different banks and account types. Additionally, certain banks may offer online account opening and closure facilities, subject to applicable regulations and security measures. Customers should refer to their bank's website or contact their bank's customer service for detailed information on account opening and closure procedures.

Deposit Schemes for N.R.I's

Non-Resident Indians (NRIs) have several options for depositing their funds in India, each with its own features, benefits, and eligibility criteria. These deposit schemes are designed to cater to the financial needs and preferences of NRIs while providing them with opportunities to earn attractive returns on their savings. Here are some common deposit schemes for NRIs in India:

NRE (Non-Resident External) Fixed Deposit:
NRE fixed deposits allow NRIs to deposit their foreign earnings in Indian rupees. Funds deposited in an NRE account are freely repatriable, meaning they can be converted back into foreign currency and transferred abroad without any restrictions.

Interest earned on NRE fixed deposits is tax-free in India. However, NRIs may be required to report this income in their country of residence and pay taxes as per local laws.

The maturity period for NRE fixed deposits typically ranges from 1 year to 10 years, with the option of both cumulative and non-cumulative interest payouts.

NRO (Non-Resident Ordinary) Fixed Deposit:

NRO fixed deposits allow NRIs to deposit income earned in India, such as rental income, dividends, or proceeds from the sale of assets. Funds deposited in an NRO account are not freely repatriable, and repatriation is subject to certain conditions and limits.

Interest earned on NRO fixed deposits is taxable in India at the prevailing rates. NRIs may also be eligible for tax benefits under the Double Taxation Avoidance Agreement (DTAA) between India and their country of residence.

The maturity period for NRO fixed deposits is similar to that of NRE fixed deposits, ranging from 1 year to 10 years, with flexible interest payout options.

FCNR (Foreign Currency Non-Resident) Deposit:

FCNR deposits allow NRIs to deposit foreign currency earnings in designated foreign currencies such as US dollars (USD), British pounds (GBP), euros (EUR), and Japanese yen (JPY).

FCNR deposits are fully repatriable, meaning both the principal amount and the interest earned can be freely converted into foreign currency and transferred abroad without any restrictions.

Interest earned on FCNR deposits is tax-free in India. However, NRIs should consult tax advisors in their country of residence for any tax implications.

NRE/NRO Savings Account:

NRIs can also open NRE or NRO savings accounts to deposit their funds in Indian rupees. These accounts offer features such as check

book facilities, ATM/debit cards, and online banking services.

Interest earned on NRE savings accounts is tax-free in India, whereas interest earned on NRO savings accounts is taxable.

Both NRE and NRO savings accounts offer repatriation benefits, allowing NRIs to transfer funds abroad subject to certain conditions and limits.

NRE/NRO Recurring Deposit:

Similar to fixed deposits, NRIs can also open recurring deposit accounts in NRE or NRO variants. These accounts allow NRIs to make regular monthly deposits and earn attractive interest rates.

NRE recurring deposits offer tax-free interest income, while NRO recurring deposits are taxable in India.

Before opting for any deposit scheme, NRIs should carefully consider factors such as interest rates, maturity periods, tax implications, repatriation restrictions, and currency risks. It's also advisable to consult with financial advisors or tax professionals to understand the implications of these deposit schemes in both India and their country of residenc.

## CHAPTER 3

BANKING INVESTMENTS

Banking investments refer to the various financial instruments and products offered by banks to individuals, businesses, and institutional investors for the purpose of generating returns on their deposited funds or invested capital. These investments typically offer varying levels of risk and return, catering to the diverse needs and preferences of investors. Here are some common banking investments:

Savings Accounts:

Savings accounts are a basic banking product that allows individuals to deposit their funds with a bank while earning interest on their balances. Savings accounts offer liquidity, safety, and ease of access to funds, making them suitable for short-term savings goals and emergency funds.

Fixed Deposits (Term Deposits):

Fixed deposits (FDs) are investment products offered by banks that allow individuals to deposit a lump sum of money for a fixed period at a predetermined interest rate. FDs offer higher interest rates compared to savings accounts and are suitable for investors looking for capital preservation and steady returns over a specific time frame.

Recurring Deposits:

Recurring deposits (RDs) are similar to fixed deposits but involve making regular monthly deposits instead of a lump sum. RDs are suitable for individuals looking to save a fixed amount of money regularly over a period to meet future financial goals.

Certificates of Deposit (CDs):

Certificates of deposit are time deposits offered by banks with fixed maturities and fixed interest rates. CDs typically offer higher interest rates than savings accounts but require the investor to commit their funds for a specific period. Early withdrawal may result in penalties.

Money Market Accounts:

Money market accounts are interest-bearing deposit accounts offered by banks that invest in low-risk, short-term securities such as Treasury bills and commercial paper. Money market accounts typically offer higher interest rates than regular savings accounts but may have higher minimum balance requirements.

Government and Municipal Bonds:

Some banks offer government and municipal bonds to investors looking for fixed-income investments. These bonds are issued by government entities and municipalities and offer regular interest payments and return of principal at maturity.

Mutual Funds:

Many banks offer mutual funds to investors, allowing them to invest in a diversified portfolio of stocks, bonds, and other securities. Mutual funds offer professional management, diversification, and liquidity, making them suitable for investors with varying risk profiles and investment goals.

Unit Linked Insurance Plans (ULIPs):

Some banks offer unit-linked insurance plans that combine investment and insurance components. ULIPs allow investors to invest in equity, debt, or hybrid funds while providing life insurance coverage.

Structured Deposits:

Structured deposits are investment products offered by banks that combine traditional deposits with derivatives. These products offer potential returns linked to the performance of underlying assets such as stocks, indices, or currencies.

Portfolio Management Services (PMS):

Some banks offer portfolio management services to high-net-worth individuals and institutional investors. PMS involves professional management of investment portfolios tailored to the investor's risk tolerance, investment objectives, and financial situation.


Before making any banking investments, individuals should carefully assess their financial goals, risk tolerance, and investment time horizon. It's advisable to diversify investments across different asset classes and seek professional financial advice if needed to make informed investment decisions. Additionally, investors should be aware of any fees, charges, and risks associated with banking investments and read the terms and conditions carefully before investing.

Negotiable instruments (NI)

Negotiable instruments (NI) are legal documents that guarantee the transfer of monetary value from one party to another. These instruments are often used in commercial transactions because they provide a convenient and secure way to transfer funds without the need for physical cash. Negotiable instruments are governed by specific laws and regulations to ensure their enforceability and facilitate their use in commerce. There are three main types of negotiable instruments:

Promissory Notes: A promissory note is a written promise by one party (the maker or issuer) to pay a specified amount of money to another party (the payee) at a predetermined future date or on demand. Promissory notes typically include details such as the amount of the loan, the interest rate (if any), the repayment terms, and the signatures of the parties involved. Promissory notes are commonly used in lending agreements, such as personal loans, business loans, and mortgages.

Bill of Exchange: A bill of exchange is a written order by one party (the drawer) to another party (the drawee) to pay a specified amount of money to a third party (the payee) at a future date or on demand. Bills of exchange are commonly used in international trade transactions, where the buyer and seller may be located in different countries and wish to use a secure payment method. Bills of exchange must meet certain legal requirements, including being signed by the drawer and containing an unconditional promise to pay.

Checks: A check is a written order by an account holder (the drawer) instructing a bank or financial institution (the drawee) to pay a specified amount of money to another party (the payee) from the drawer's account. Checks are widely used for making payments and transferring funds in both personal and business transactions. Checks must be signed by the drawer and contain essential details such as the payee's name, the amount to be paid, the date, and the account number.

Negotiable instruments have several key characteristics that make them valuable in commercial transactions:

Transferability: Negotiable instruments are freely transferable from one party to another through endorsement and delivery. The holder of a negotiable instrument can transfer ownership to another party, who then becomes entitled to the rights and obligations under the instrument.

Holder in Due Course: A holder in due course is a party who acquires a negotiable instrument in good faith, for value, and without notice of any defects or defenses. Holders in due course have certain legal rights and protections, including the right to enforce the instrument against the parties liable on it.

Enforceability: Negotiable instruments are legally enforceable documents, meaning that the parties involved are legally obligated to fulfill their obligations under the instrument. Courts will generally enforce negotiable instruments according to their terms, provided that they meet the legal requirements for negotiability.

Uniformity: Negotiable instruments are subject to uniform rules and regulations, which provide consistency and predictability in their use and interpretation. These rules are codified in laws such as the Uniform Commercial Code (UCC) in the United States and similar statutes in other jurisdictions.

Overall, negotiable instruments play a crucial role in facilitating commercial transactions by providing a secure and efficient means of transferring funds and ensuring the enforceability of payment obligations between parties.

Types parties to NI's

Negotiable instruments (NIs) involve various parties, each with distinct roles and responsibilities. The types of parties to negotiable instruments typically include:

Drawer: The drawer is the party who creates and signs the negotiable instrument, instructing the drawee to pay a specified amount of money to the payee. In the case of a check, the drawer is the account holder who writes and signs the check.

Drawee: The drawee is the party upon whom the order to pay is made. This could be a bank or financial institution in the case of a check, or any entity capable of making payments, such as an individual or another business.

Payee: The payee is the party to whom payment is to be made. The payee is typically named on the negotiable instrument and is entitled to receive the specified amount of money upon.

Endorser: An endorser is a party who signs the back of the negotiable instrument, thereby transferring ownership or rights to another party. Endorsement can be blank (simply signing the back) or special (naming a specific endorsee).

Endorsee: An endorsee is the party to whom an instrument is endorsed, thereby transferring ownership or rights to that party. The endorsee becomes the new holder of the instrument and may further negotiate or enforce it.

Holder: The holder of a negotiable instrument is the party who is in possession of the instrument and entitled to enforce its terms. The holder may be the payee, endorsee, or subsequent transferee who acquires the instrument through negotiation.

Acceptor: In the case of a bill of exchange, the acceptor is the drawee who agrees to pay the specified amount of money to the payee. Acceptance typically involves writing the word "accepted" and signing the bill.

Maker: In the case of a promissory note, the maker is the party who promises to pay a specified amount of money to the payee. The maker creates and signs the promissory note, thereby assuming the obligation to repay the debt.

Principal: The principal is the original amount of money specified in the negotiable instrument, which is to be paid to the payee upon presentation of the instrument.

Co-maker/Guarantor: In some cases, a third party may also be involved in a negotiable instrument as a co-maker or guarantor, providing additional assurance of payment if the primary party (maker or drawer) fails to fulfill their obligation.

These parties play essential roles in the creation, negotiation, and enforcement of negotiable instruments, ensuring the smooth functioning of commercial transactions and the transfer of funds between parties.

Crossing, Endorsements, Payments and Collection of Cheques, Bouncing of Cheques
Crossing of Cheques:
Crossing of cheques is a security measure used to prevent the unauthorized transfer of funds and reduce the risk of fraud. When a cheque is crossed, it means that the cheque can only be credited to the account of the payee and cannot be encashed over the counter.
There are two types of crossing: General Crossing and Special Crossing.

General Crossing: Two parallel lines are drawn across the face of the cheque, with or without the words "& Co." or "Account Payee Only". This indicates that the cheque can only be deposited into the payee's bank account.

Special Crossing: In addition to the parallel lines, the name of a bank or "not negotiable" may be added between the lines. This directs the cheque to be deposited only into the specified bank account.

Endorsements of Cheques:

Endorsement refers to the signing of the back of a cheque by the payee, thereby transferring the right to receive the payment to another person or entity.

Different types of endorsements include Blank Endorsement, Special Endorsement, Restrictive Endorsement, and Conditional Endorsement.

Payments and Collection of Cheques:

When a cheque is deposited into a bank account, the bank collects the funds from the drawer's account and credits it to the payee's account. This process is known as cheque collection.

The time taken for cheque clearance and crediting of funds depends on factors such as the location of the banks, type of cheque (local or outstation), and clearing cycle.

Bouncing of Cheques:

A bounced cheque, also known as a dishonored or returned cheque, occurs when the cheque cannot be honored by the drawer's bank due to insufficient funds, a frozen account, or other reasons.

When a cheque bounces, it is returned unpaid to the payee's bank along with a reason code indicating the cause of dishonor.

Consequences of bouncing a cheque may include penalties, legal action, damage to the drawer's credit rating, and loss of trust and reputation.

These banking terms are essential to understand for anyone dealing with cheque transactions, whether as a payer or payee. Adhering to proper procedures and regulations helps ensure the smooth processing of cheques and mitigates the risk of fraud or financial loss.

Implications

Crossing of Cheques:

Implication: Crossing of cheques enhances the security of transactions by ensuring that the payment is made only to the intended payee's bank account.

Benefit: Reduces the risk of fraudulent encashment and unauthorized diversion of funds.

Compliance: Banks and individuals are required to adhere to crossing instructions specified on cheques to ensure proper handling and crediting of funds.

Endorsements of Cheques:

Implication: Endorsements facilitate the transfer of ownership and rights to receive payment from one party to another.

Benefit: Enables flexibility in cheque transactions, allowing payees to transfer funds to third parties or financial institutions.

Compliance: Endorsements must comply with legal requirements and banking regulations to ensure the validity and enforceability of the endorsement.

Payments and Collection of Cheques:

Implication: Timely clearance and crediting of funds are essential for smooth and efficient cheque transactions.

Benefit: Facilitates the flow of funds between payers and payees, supporting economic activities and financial transactions.

Compliance: Banks and financial institutions must adhere to established clearing and settlement processes to ensure the integrity and efficiency of cheque collection.

Bouncing of Cheques:

Implication: Bounced cheques can have financial, legal, and reputational consequences for both the drawer and the payee.

Consequences: The drawer may face penalties, legal action, and damage to credit rating, while the payee may experience financial loss and inconvenience.

Compliance: Both drawers and payees are responsible for ensuring sufficient funds and proper management of bank accounts to avoid bouncing of cheques and associated consequences.

Understanding the implications of these banking concepts is crucial for individuals, businesses, and financial institutions involved in cheque transactions. Adherence to legal and regulatory requirements, as well as best practices in cheque handling, helps promote transparency, reliability, and trust in the banking system.

Various Laws Affecting Bankers

Bankers are subject to various laws and regulations that govern their operations, transactions, and interactions with customers. These laws are designed to ensure the stability, integrity, and fairness of the banking system and to protect the interests of depositors, borrowers, and other stakeholders. Some of the key laws affecting bankers include:

Banking Regulation Act, 1949:

The Banking Regulation Act, 1949, is the primary legislation governing the banking sector in India. It provides a comprehensive regulatory framework for the establishment, operation, and regulation of banks in the country.

The Act empowers the Reserve Bank of India (RBI) to regulate and supervise banks, issue banking licenses, prescribe prudential norms, and oversee banking operations to maintain financial stability and protect depositors' interests.

Reserve Bank of India Act, 1934:

The Reserve Bank of India Act, 1934, establishes the Reserve Bank of India (RBI) as the central bank of the country and outlines its powers, functions, and responsibilities.

The Act empowers the RBI to formulate and implement monetary policy, regulate the banking and financial system, issue currency, manage foreign exchange reserves, and promote the stability of the financial system.

Negotiable Instruments Act, 1881:

The Negotiable Instruments Act, 1881, governs the use, issuance, and transfer of negotiable instruments such as promissory notes, bills of exchange, and cheques.

Bankers frequently deal with negotiable instruments in their day-to-day operations, and the Act provides legal provisions for the enforcement of rights and obligations related to such instruments.

Foreign Exchange Management Act (FEMA), 1999:

FEMA regulates foreign exchange transactions and transactions involving foreign currency in India. It aims to facilitate external trade and payments, promote orderly development and maintenance of the foreign exchange market, and conserve foreign exchange reserves.

Bankers dealing with foreign exchange transactions, cross-border trade, and international banking operations must comply with FEMA regulations and reporting requirements.

Securitization and Reconstruction of Financial Assets and Enforcement of Security Interest (SARFAESI) Act, 2002:

The SARFAESI Act empowers banks and financial institutions to enforce the security interest in defaulted loans and recover dues from borrowers without court intervention.

Banks use the provisions of the SARFAESI Act to take possession of collateral assets, sell or lease them, and recover outstanding loan amounts in cases of default.

Prevention of Money Laundering Act (PMLA), 2002:

The PMLA aims to prevent money laundering and the financing of terrorism by imposing obligations on banks and other financial institutions to implement customer due diligence measures, maintain records, and report suspicious transactions to the authorities.

Banks are required to establish robust anti-money laundering (AML) and know your customer (KYC) procedures to comply with the provisions of the PMLA.

Consumer Protection Act, 2019:

The Consumer Protection Act, 2019, provides a legal framework for the protection of consumer rights and interests, including those related to banking and financial services.

Banks are required to adhere to fair practices, provide transparent disclosure of terms and conditions, and address customer grievances effectively to comply with consumer protection regulations.

These are some of the key laws and regulations that affect bankers and banking operations in India. Compliance with these laws is essential for banks to operate legally, maintain public trust, and contribute to the stability and efficiency of the financial system.

CHAPTER4

BANKING SERVICES

Banking services encompass a wide range of financial products and facilities offered by banks and other financial institutions to individuals, businesses, and governments. These services are designed to meet the diverse financial needs and requirements of customers and facilitate various monetary transactions. Here are some common banking services:

Deposit Services:

Savings Accounts: Basic deposit accounts that offer interest on deposited funds and provide easy access to funds for day-to-day transactions.

Current Accounts: Transactional accounts primarily used by businesses and organizations for frequent transactions, with features such as checkbooks, overdraft facilities, and online banking.

Fixed Deposits: Time deposits where funds are deposited for a fixed term at a predetermined interest rate, offering higher interest rates compared to savings accounts.

Loan and Credit Services:

Personal Loans: Unsecured loans provided to individuals for various purposes such as home renovations, medical expenses, or debt consolidation.

Home Loans: Loans provided to individuals for purchasing, constructing, or renovating residential properties, with the property serving as collateral.

Auto Loans: Loans provided for purchasing vehicles, with the vehicle itself serving as collateral.

Business Loans: Loans provided to businesses for various purposes such as working capital, expansion, or purchasing equipment.

Credit Cards: Revolving lines of credit that allow customers to make purchases, withdraw cash, and access credit facilities based on their creditworthiness.

Investment Services:

Mutual Funds: Investment products that pool funds from multiple investors to invest in diversified portfolios of stocks, bonds, or other securities.

Fixed Income Products: Investment options such as government bonds, corporate bonds, and debentures that offer fixed interest payments over a specified period.

Equity Trading: Services for buying and selling stocks and shares listed on stock exchanges, enabling investors to participate in the equity markets.

Insurance Products: Insurance policies offered by banks or in collaboration with insurance companies, including life insurance, health insurance, and general insurance.

Payment and Transfer Services:

Online Banking: Internet-based banking services that allow customers to access their accounts, make payments, transfer funds, and perform other transactions remotely.

Mobile Banking: Banking services accessible through mobile devices, enabling customers to conduct transactions on the go.

Electronic Funds Transfer (EFT): Services for transferring funds electronically between bank accounts, including NEFT, RTGS, IMPS, and UPI.

Cheque Processing: Services for clearing and processing cheques, including check deposits, cheque issuance, and cheque truncation.

Wealth Management and Advisory Services:

Financial Planning: Services for assessing individuals' financial goals, creating personalized financial plans, and providing guidance on investment and wealth management strategies.

Portfolio Management: Professional management of investment portfolios on behalf of clients, including asset allocation, risk management, and investment decision-making.

Forex and International Banking Services:

Foreign Exchange (Forex) Services: Facilities for buying and selling foreign currency, remittance services, and foreign exchange hedging solutions.

International Trade Finance: Services for facilitating international trade transactions, including letters of credit, export financing, and import financing.

Specialized Banking Services:

Private Banking: Tailored banking services for high-net-worth individuals, including personalized wealth management, investment advisory, and concierge services.

Corporate Banking: Banking services tailored for corporate clients, including cash management, trade finance, and treasury services.

Retail Banking: Banking services targeted at individual consumers, including retail lending, deposit services, and personalized financial advice.

These are some of the common banking services offered by banks and financial institutions worldwide. The availability and scope of banking services may vary depending on the institution, regulatory environment, and customer requirements.

Banking Services and Processes

Safe Custody:

Definition: Safe custody services involve banks providing secure storage facilities for valuable documents, securities, and other items on behalf of customers.

Features: Banks offer lockers or safe deposit vaults equipped with high- security measures such as biometric access, CCTV surveillance, and dual key control.

Benefits: Safe custody services protect valuable items from loss, theft, or damage and provide customers with peace of mind knowing their assets are stored securely.

MICR Clearing (Magnetic Ink Character Recognition):

Definition: MICR clearing is a process used by banks to facilitate the clearance of cheques through automated systems.

Features: Cheques are printed with MICR codes at the bottom, which contain information such as bank branch, account number, and cheque number in a machine-readable format.

Benefits: MICR clearing speeds up the processing and settlement of cheques, reduces manual errors, and enhances the efficiency of the banking system.

ATMs (Automated Teller Machines):

Definition: ATMs are self-service banking terminals that allow customers to perform various banking transactions without visiting a branch.

Features: ATMs enable cash withdrawals, account inquiries, fund transfers, bill payments, and other transactions using debit cards or credit cards.

Benefits: ATMs provide convenient access to banking services 24/7, reduce the need for branch visits, and offer flexibility and accessibility for customers.

Credit Cards:

Definition: Credit cards are payment cards issued by banks that allow cardholders to borrow funds from the issuing bank to make purchases or withdraw cash.

Features: Credit cards offer a revolving line of credit, allowing cardholders to pay off balances over time, with interest charged on outstanding balances.

Benefits: Credit cards provide convenient payment options, rewards, cashback offers, and purchase protection features, enhancing the purchasing power and financial flexibility of cardholders.

Debit Cards:

Definition: Debit cards are payment cards linked to a bank account, allowing cardholders to make purchases or withdraw cash directly from their account balance.

Features: Debit cards deduct the purchase amount directly from the cardholder's account, without incurring debt or interest charges.

Benefits: Debit cards offer convenient access to funds, eliminate the need to carry cash, and provide security features such as PIN authentication and transaction alerts.

Traveler's Cheques:

Definition: Traveler's cheques are prepaid instruments issued by banks or financial institutions, designed to provide a secure and convenient way for travelers to carry money while traveling abroad.

Features: Traveler's cheques can be used to make purchases, pay for services, or exchange for local currency at designated locations worldwide.

Benefits: Traveler's cheques offer security against loss or theft, as they can be replaced if lost or stolen, and provide peace of mind for travelers concerned about carrying large amounts of cash.

Banking Ombudsman and Customer Services:

Definition: Banking Ombudsman is an independent dispute resolution mechanism established by the Reserve Bank of India (RBI) to address complaints and grievances of bank customers.

Features: The Banking Ombudsman investigates and resolves complaints related to deficiency in banking services, unfair practices, or non-compliance with banking regulations.

Benefits: Banking Ombudsman provides a recourse for customers to seek redressal for their grievances, promotes transparency and accountability in the banking sector, and enhances customer confidence and trust.

Fraud Detection and Control:

Definition: Fraud detection and control mechanisms are implemented by banks to identify, prevent, and mitigate fraudulent activities such as unauthorized transactions, identity theft, and financial scams.

Features: Banks use advanced technology, data analytics, and risk management techniques to detect suspicious activities, monitor transactions in real-time, and implement security protocols to protect customer accounts and assets.

Benefits: Fraud detection and control measures help safeguard the integrity of the banking system, protect customer funds, and maintain trust and confidence in the banking sector.

These banking services and processes play a crucial role in meeting the financial needs of customers, ensuring the smooth functioning of the banking system, and promoting trust and confidence in financial institutions.

CHAPTER 5

EMERGING TRENDS AND ISSUES IN BANKING INDUSTRY

Emerging trends and issues in the banking industry reflect the evolving landscape shaped by technological advancements, changing customer preferences, regulatory developments, and economic shifts. Here are some notable trends and issues currently influencing the banking sector:

Digital Transformation:

Banks are increasingly adopting digital technologies to enhance customer experience, streamline operations, and drive innovation.

Digital banking platforms, mobile apps, and online services enable customers to access banking services conveniently from anywhere, anytime.

Fintech Disruption:

The rise of fintech startups is challenging traditional banking models by offering innovative solutions in areas such as payments, lending, wealth management, and insurance.

Banks are collaborating with fintech firms through partnerships, investments, or in-house innovation labs to leverage their expertise and stay competitive.

Open Banking:

Open banking initiatives are promoting greater transparency, competition, and collaboration in the banking industry by allowing customers to share their financial data securely with third-party providers.

APIs (Application Programming Interfaces) enable banks to integrate with third-party services, offering customers access to a wider range of financial products and personalized solutions.

Data Analytics and AI:

Banks are leveraging big data analytics and artificial intelligence (AI) to gain insights into customer behavior, improve risk management, and enhance decision-making processes.

AI-powered chatbots and virtual assistants are being deployed to provide personalized customer support, automate routine tasks, and deliver proactive financial advice.

Cybersecurity Threats:

The increasing digitization of banking services has led to a rise in cybersecurity threats such as data breaches, phishing attacks, ransomware, and malware.

Banks are investing in robust cybersecurity measures, including encryption, multi-factor authentication, threat detection systems, and employee training, to safeguard customer data and mitigate cyber risks.

Regulatory Compliance:

Banks face a complex regulatory environment with evolving compliance requirements, including anti-money laundering (AML), know your customer (KYC), data protection, and consumer protection regulations.

Compliance costs are increasing, and banks need to invest in technology and expertise to ensure adherence to regulatory standards and avoid penalties.

Sustainability and ESG:

Environmental, social, and governance (ESG) factors are gaining prominence in banking, with growing investor and consumer demand for sustainable and responsible banking practices.

Banks are integrating ESG considerations into their lending decisions, investment strategies, and risk management frameworks to address climate change, social inequalities, and ethical concerns.

Shift to Remote Work:

The COVID-19 pandemic has accelerated the adoption of remote work practices in the banking industry, prompting banks to reevaluate their business continuity plans, digital infrastructure, and employee engagement strategies.

Remote work arrangements have implications for cybersecurity, collaboration, productivity, and talent management in the banking sector.

These emerging trends and issues are reshaping the banking industry, driving transformation, innovation, and adaptation to meet the evolving needs of customers and stakeholders in a rapidly changing environment.

International Banking

International banking refers to the provision of banking services across national borders, involving financial institutions that operate in multiple countries or cater to clients engaged in international transactions. International banking plays a crucial role in facilitating global trade, investment, and financial flows, and it encompasses various activities and services tailored to the needs of multinational corporations, financial institutions, governments, and individuals engaged in cross-border activities. Here are some key aspects of international banking:

Cross-Border Transactions: International banks facilitate cross-border transactions, including trade finance, foreign exchange transactions, remittances, and international wire transfers. These services help businesses and individuals conduct transactions in different currencies and across multiple jurisdictions, supporting global commerce and investment.

Foreign Currency Services: International banks provide foreign currency services, allowing clients to hold accounts, make payments, and conduct transactions in foreign currencies. These services help manage currency risk and facilitate international trade and investment activities.

Trade Finance: International banks offer trade finance services, such as letters of credit, trade financing, and export/import financing, to facilitate international trade transactions. These services provide financing and risk mitigation tools to exporters and importers, enabling them to engage in cross-border trade with confidence.

Corporate Banking: International banks provide a range of corporate banking services to multinational corporations, including cash management, treasury services, corporate lending, and investment banking. These services support the financial needs of corporate clients operating in multiple countries and help optimize their capital, liquidity, and risk management.

Wealth Management: International banks offer wealth management and private banking services to high-net-worth individuals and families with global financial interests. These services include investment advisory, asset management, estate planning, and tax optimization solutions tailored to the unique needs of international clients.

Correspondent Banking: International banks maintain correspondent banking relationships with financial institutions in other countries, enabling them to provide services such as clearing, settlement, and payment processing for cross-border transactions. Correspondent banking facilitates international trade and financial transactions by providing access to local banking systems and networks.

Regulatory Compliance: International banks must comply with a complex regulatory framework that includes laws and regulations in multiple jurisdictions, as well as international standards and guidelines set by organizations such as the Financial Action Task Force (FATF) and the Basel Committee on Banking Supervision. Compliance with regulatory requirements is essential to mitigate legal, regulatory, and reputational risks associated with cross-border banking activities.

Risk Management: International banks engage in comprehensive risk management practices to identify, assess, and mitigate risks associated with cross-border activities, including credit risk, market risk, liquidity risk, operational risk, and compliance risk. Robust risk management frameworks are essential to maintain the safety, soundness, and stability of international banking operations.

Overall, international banking plays a vital role in supporting global economic integration, facilitating cross-border transactions, and meeting the financial needs of clients engaged in international trade, investment, and finance.

Euro Banks and Offshore Banking

Euro banks and offshore banking are two distinct but interconnected aspects of international banking, each serving specific purposes in the global financial system:

Euro banks are financial institutions that operate within the Eurozone, which consists of countries that have adopted the euro as their official currency. These banks play a central role in facilitating financial transactions, providing banking services, and supporting economic activity within the Eurozone countries. Key features of euro banks include:

Eurozone Membership: Euro banks are located in countries that are part of the Eurozone, such as Germany, France, Italy, and Spain. They conduct business and operate their banking activities in euros, the common currency of the Eurozone.

European Central Bank (ECB) Oversight: Euro banks are subject to regulatory oversight by the European Central Bank (ECB) and national banking authorities within the Eurozone. The ECB sets monetary policy, supervises banking activities, and ensures the stability of the euro currency.

Cross-Border Transactions: Euro banks facilitate cross-border transactions within the Eurozone, allowing businesses and individuals to make payments, transfers, and investments across different countries using the euro currency.

Capital Markets Integration: Euro banks are part of an integrated European financial system that includes capital markets, securities exchanges, and financial infrastructure. They provide access to capital markets, funding sources, and financial instruments for businesses, governments, and investors within the Eurozone.

Euro Clearing and Settlement: Euro banks serve as clearing and settlement agents for euro-denominated transactions, providing services such as payment processing, securities settlement, and collateral management for financial transactions conducted within the Eurozone.

Offshore Banking:

Offshore banking refers to banking activities conducted in jurisdictions outside the depositor's country of residence or domicile, often in low-tax or tax-neutral jurisdictions known as offshore financial centers (OFCs). Offshore banking serves various purposes, including tax optimization, asset protection, privacy, and diversification of financial holdings. Key features of offshore banking include:

Tax Optimization: Offshore banks offer tax-efficient banking and investment solutions for individuals and businesses seeking to minimize their tax liabilities, preserve wealth, and optimize their financial affairs.

Confidentiality and Privacy: Offshore banks provide a high level of confidentiality and privacy for their clients, often through strict bank secrecy laws and regulations that protect the identity and financial information of account holders.

Asset Protection: Offshore banking jurisdictions offer legal and financial structures, such as trusts, foundations, and offshore companies, that provide asset protection and wealth preservation benefits for individuals and families seeking to shield their assets from creditors, lawsuits, or other risks.

Diversification and Internationalization: Offshore banking allows individuals and businesses to diversify their financial holdings and access international markets, currencies, and investment opportunities outside their home country.

Global Financial Services: Offshore banks offer a wide range of global financial services, including banking, investment management, wealth planning, estate administration, and fiduciary services, tailored to the needs of international clients.

Regulatory Oversight: Offshore banking jurisdictions are subject to regulation and supervision by local financial authorities, as well as international standards and best practices for anti-money laundering (AML), know-your-customer (KYC), and combating the financing of terrorism (CFT).

Compliance and Transparency: Offshore banks must comply with regulatory requirements and international standards for transparency, disclosure, and reporting, including tax information exchange agreements (TIEAs) and common reporting standards (CRS) aimed at preventing tax evasion and promoting financial transparency.

Overall, Euro banks and offshore banking serve distinct but complementary roles in the global financial system, providing banking services, financial solutions, and opportunities for individuals, businesses, and investors to manage their finances, optimize their tax positions, and achieve their financial objectives within the context of regional and international regulations and market dynamics.

## CHAPTER 6

BANKING RISKS

Banking risks encompass a wide range of potential threats and uncertainties that banks face in their day-to-day operations and strategic decision-making processes. Understanding and managing these risks are essential for ensuring the stability, profitability, and resilience of banking institutions. Here's an overview of the key categories of banking risks:

Credit Risk:

Credit risk arises from the possibility that borrowers may default on their obligations, resulting in losses for the bank. This risk is inherent in lending activities and includes the risk of non-payment, delayed payment, or deterioration in the creditworthiness of borrowers.

Banks assess credit risk through credit analysis, credit scoring, and collateral evaluation, and manage it through prudent underwriting standards, loan diversification, and risk-based pricing.

Market Risk:

Market risk stems from fluctuations in financial markets, including interest rates, foreign exchange rates, equity prices, and commodity prices. It encompasses the risk of losses arising from adverse movements in market variables that affect the value of banks' assets, liabilities, and off-balance-sheet exposures.

Banks manage market risk through hedging strategies, diversification of investment portfolios, stress testing, and scenario analysis.

Liquidity Risk:

Liquidity risk arises from the inability of banks to meet their short-term funding obligations or to convert assets into cash quickly without incurring significant losses. It includes funding liquidity risk (inability to obtain funding) and market liquidity risk (illiquidity in financial markets).

Banks manage liquidity risk by maintaining sufficient liquidity buffers, diversifying funding sources, monitoring cash flows, and participating in central bank liquidity facilities.

Operational Risk:

Operational risk arises from the potential for losses resulting from inadequate or failed internal processes, systems, people, or external events. It includes risks related to technology failures, fraud, human error, legal and regulatory compliance, and business continuity.

Banks mitigate operational risk through robust internal controls, automation of processes, employee training, cybersecurity measures, and contingency planning.

Compliance and Regulatory Risk:

Compliance and regulatory risk arises from the failure to comply with laws, regulations, and industry standards governing banking activities. Non- compliance can result in financial penalties, reputational damage, legal liabilities, and restrictions on business operations.

Banks manage compliance risk through comprehensive compliance programs, regulatory oversight, internal audits, and continuous monitoring of regulatory developments.

Reputational Risk:

Reputational risk arises from negative perceptions or public backlash resulting from the bank's actions, behaviors, or associations. It can stem from unethical conduct, poor customer service, controversies, or adverse media coverage.

Banks protect their reputation through ethical conduct, transparency, stakeholder engagement, social responsibility initiatives, and effective crisis management strategies.

Strategic Risk:

Strategic risk arises from the potential failure of business strategies, decisions, or initiatives to achieve desired objectives or to adapt to changes in the competitive environment, technological advancements, or market dynamics.

Banks manage strategic risk through robust strategic planning processes, scenario analysis, risk appetite frameworks, and ongoing performance monitoring and evaluation.

Cybersecurity Risk:

Cybersecurity risk arises from the threat of cyber attacks, data breaches, and information security incidents that can compromise the confidentiality, integrity, and availability of banks' systems, data, and customer information.

Banks address cybersecurity risk through robust IT security measures, encryption, network monitoring, employee training, incident response plans, and collaboration with industry partners and cybersecurity experts.

Environmental and Social Risk:

Environmental and social risk arises from the bank's exposure to environmental degradation, climate change, social inequalities, human rights violations, and other sustainability-related issues associated with its lending, investment, and business activities.

Banks manage environmental and social risk through ESG (environmental, social, and governance) integration, responsible lending practices, sustainable finance initiatives, and stakeholder engagement.

Effective risk management is essential for banks to identify, assess, mitigate, and monitor these risks, ensuring the safety and soundness of the banking system, protecting stakeholders' interests, and maintaining trust and confidence in financial institutions.

Corporate Governance

Corporate governance refers to the system of rules, practices, processes, and structures by which companies are directed, controlled, and managed. It encompasses the relationships and responsibilities among various stakeholders, including shareholders, the board of directors, management, employees, customers, suppliers, and the broader community. Effective corporate governance aims to promote transparency, accountability, integrity, and ethical

conduct       within organizations, ultimately       enhancing       long-term       value
creation       and sustainability. Here are key components and principles of corporate
governance:

Board of Directors:

The board of directors plays a central role in corporate governance, providing oversight, guidance, and strategic direction to the company.

The board is responsible for appointing and overseeing executive management, setting corporate objectives and policies, monitoring performance, and safeguarding shareholders' interests.

Boards should be composed of a diverse mix of independent, competent, and experienced directors with a range of skills and expertise relevant to the company's business and industry.

Shareholder Rights:

Shareholders have certain rights and responsibilities that should be respected and protected by the company's management and board of directors.

These rights include the right to vote on significant corporate decisions, elect directors, receive information and financial reports, and participate in shareholder meetings.

Companies should foster open communication with shareholders and ensure transparency in their dealings to uphold shareholder rights and promote investor confidence.

Ethical Conduct and Corporate Culture:

Ethical conduct and a strong corporate culture are essential for maintaining trust, integrity, and reputation within organizations.

Companies should establish a code of ethics and conduct that sets out expected standards of behavior for directors, executives, employees, and other stakeholders.

Promoting a culture of integrity, honesty, respect, and accountability throughout the organization helps mitigate risks, foster employee engagement, and build stakeholder trust.

Risk Management and Internal Controls:

Effective risk management and internal control systems are critical for identifying, assessing, mitigating, and monitoring risks that could impact the company's objectives and performance.

Companies should establish robust risk management frameworks, policies, and procedures to manage various risks, including financial, operational, compliance, strategic, and reputational risks.

Internal controls should be implemented to ensure compliance with laws, regulations, and internal policies, safeguard assets, prevent fraud and errors, and enhance operational efficiency.

Transparency and Disclosure:

Transparency and disclosure are essential for providing stakeholders with accurate, timely, and relevant information about the company's financial performance, operations, strategies, risks, and governance practices.

Companies should adhere to disclosure requirements mandated by regulatory authorities and stock exchanges and go beyond minimum disclosure standards to provide comprehensive and meaningful information to stakeholders.

Transparent communication fosters investor confidence, enhances market efficiency, and enables stakeholders to make informed decisions about the company.

Stakeholder Engagement:

Companies should engage with a broad range of stakeholders, including shareholders, employees, customers, suppliers, regulators, and the community, to understand their interests, concerns, and expectations.

Effective stakeholder engagement fosters mutual trust, collaboration, and long-term relationships, leading to better decision-making, risk management, and value creation for all stakeholders.

Companies should establish mechanisms for receiving feedback, addressing stakeholder grievances, and integrating stakeholder perspectives into corporate strategies and decision-making processes.

Board Committees:

Boards typically establish committees to assist in fulfilling their oversight responsibilities in key areas such as audit, risk management, compensation, nomination and governance, and sustainability.

These committees are composed of independent directors with relevant expertise and are tasked with reviewing, analyzing, and making recommendations on specific issues within their mandate.

Committee structures and charters should be designed to ensure independence, effectiveness, and alignment with the company's objectives and regulatory requirements.

Corporate Social Responsibility (CSR):

Corporate social responsibility involves integrating environmental, social, and ethical considerations into the company's business operations and interactions with stakeholders.

Companies should identify and address social and environmental impacts associated with their activities, products, and services, and contribute to sustainable development and societal well-being.

CSR initiatives can encompass areas such as environmental stewardship, community engagement, philanthropy, employee welfare, and responsible sourcing, and should be aligned with the company's values and business strategy.

Effective corporate governance practices promote transparency, accountability, integrity, and sustainability, enhancing trust and confidence among stakeholders and contributing to the long-term success and resilience of organizations. By adhering to principles of good governance, companies can mitigate risks, seize opportunities, and create value for shareholders and society as a whole.

Credit Risk Management in Banks

Credit risk management is a critical function in banks that involves assessing, mitigating, and monitoring the risks associated with lending activities and credit exposures. Effective credit risk management helps banks make informed decisions about extending credit, managing their loan portfolios, and safeguarding against potential losses. Here are key components and strategies involved in credit risk management in banks:

Credit Policies and Procedures: Banks establish comprehensive credit policies and procedures that define the criteria for lending decisions, including credit underwriting standards, risk appetite, loan approval processes, and portfolio management guidelines. These policies ensure consistency, transparency, and compliance with regulatory requirements.

Credit Assessment and Analysis: Banks conduct thorough credit assessments and analysis of borrowers' creditworthiness, financial condition, repayment capacity, and collateral to evaluate the risks associated with lending. This involves gathering and analyzing financial statements, credit reports, cash flow projections, and other relevant information to assess the borrower's ability and willingness to repay the loan.

Credit Scoring and Rating Models: Banks utilize credit scoring and rating models to quantify and classify the credit risk of borrowers based on various risk factors, such as credit history, income stability, debt-to-income ratio, and industry sector. These models help standardize credit evaluation processes, improve risk assessment accuracy, and facilitate decision-making.

Risk-Based Pricing: Banks employ risk-based pricing strategies to adjust interest rates, fees, and terms based on the credit risk profile of borrowers. Higher-risk borrowers may be charged higher interest rates or required to provide additional collateral or guarantees to compensate for the increased credit risk.

Credit Limits and Exposure Management: Banks establish credit limits for individual borrowers and counterparties to control their credit exposure and concentration risk. Limits may be based on factors such as borrower creditworthiness, industry sector, geographic location, and collateral value. Banks monitor credit limits regularly and adjust them as needed to mitigate excessive risk exposure.

Collateral and Security: Banks may require borrowers to provide collateral or security to mitigate credit risk and secure repayment of loans. Collateral may include real estate, inventory, equipment, accounts receivable, or other assets that can be liquidated in the event of default. Banks assess the quality, value, and enforceability of collateral to ensure adequate protection against potential losses.

Loan Covenants and Conditions: Banks impose loan covenants and conditions to mitigate credit risk and protect their interests. These covenants may include requirements for financial reporting, maintenance of certain financial ratios, restrictions on additional debt issuance, and prohibitions on asset sales or dividend payments that could impair loan repayment.

Credit Monitoring and Portfolio Management: Banks continuously monitor credit exposures, loan performance, and portfolio quality to identify early warning signs of credit deterioration, delinquencies, or defaults. They employ risk management tools, such as credit risk reports, stress testing, scenario analysis, and credit risk models, to assess portfolio risk, measure credit losses, and proactively manage credit risk.

Provisioning and Loss Reserves: Banks set aside provisions and establish loss reserves to cover expected credit losses and impairments in their loan portfolios. They adhere to regulatory requirements and accounting standards, such as the International Financial Reporting Standards (IFRS) and the Basel III framework, for calculating and reporting credit provisions and reserves. Credit Risk Mitigation Techniques: Banks employ various credit risk mitigation techniques, such as credit derivatives, credit insurance, loan syndications, securitization, and loan sales, to transfer, hedge, or diversify credit risk exposures. These techniques help banks manage credit risk more effectively and optimize their capital allocation and risk-adjusted returns.

Overall, effective credit risk management is essential for banks to maintain financial stability, profitability, and resilience in the face of evolving market conditions, economic uncertainties, and regulatory requirements. By adopting sound credit risk management practices, banks can mitigate credit losses, preserve capital, and build trust and confidence among stakeholders, including depositors, investors, and regulators.

Liquidity Risk Management

Liquidity risk management is the process of identifying, assessing, monitoring, and mitigating the risk of being unable to meet short-term funding obligations or convert assets into cash quickly without incurring significant losses. It is a critical aspect of bank management and involves ensuring that a bank has access to sufficient liquidity to meet its operational needs, honor deposit withdrawals, and fulfill other financial obligations as they arise. Here's an overview of liquidity risk management:

Types of Liquidity Risk:
Funding Liquidity Risk: Arises from the inability to obtain funds to meet short-term obligations as they come due, resulting in liquidity shortfalls.
Market Liquidity Risk: Arises from the inability to sell assets or unwind positions quickly at fair market prices due to illiquidity in financial markets or disruptions in trading activity.
Identification and Assessment:
Banks identify and assess liquidity risk by analyzing their funding sources, cash flows, maturity profiles, and liquidity buffers.

Stress testing and scenario analysis are used to evaluate the potential impact of adverse liquidity shocks, such as sudden deposit withdrawals, market disruptions, or funding freezes.

Monitoring and Measurement:

Banks monitor liquidity metrics and indicators on an ongoing basis to track their liquidity position and identify emerging risks.

Key liquidity measures include liquidity coverage ratio (LCR), net stable funding ratio (NSFR), cash flow projections, funding concentration, and market liquidity metrics.

Liquidity Risk Policies and Limits:

Banks establish liquidity risk management policies, procedures, and limits to govern their liquidity risk-taking activities.

Liquidity risk limits are set based on regulatory requirements, internal risk appetite, liquidity stress testing results, and business strategy considerations.

Liquidity Risk Mitigation Strategies:

Banks employ various strategies to mitigate liquidity risk and enhance their liquidity resilience, including:

Maintaining Adequate Liquidity Buffers: Holding sufficient high- quality liquid assets (HQLA) to meet short-term funding needs and regulatory requirements.

Diversifying Funding Sources: Relying on a mix of stable and diversified funding sources, including retail deposits, wholesale funding, interbank borrowing, and capital markets funding.

Establishing Contingency Funding Plans: Developing contingency funding plans (CFPs) to outline strategies and actions to be taken in response to liquidity stress events.

Accessing Central Bank Facilities: Utilizing central bank facilities, such as discount windows, standing facilities, and emergency liquidity assistance (ELA), as a last resort source of funding during liquidity crises.

Implementing Collateralized Funding Arrangements: Entering into collateralized funding arrangements, such as repurchase agreements (repos) or securities lending, to access additional liquidity secured by eligible collateral.

Regulatory Requirements:

Banks are subject to regulatory requirements and standards related to liquidity risk management, such as the Basel III liquidity framework established by the Basel Committee on Banking Supervision (BCBS).

Regulatory liquidity ratios, such as the liquidity coverage ratio (LCR) and net stable funding ratio (NSFR), impose minimum liquidity requirements on banks to ensure their resilience to liquidity stress events.

Governance and Oversight:

Effective governance and oversight of liquidity risk management are essential for ensuring accountability, transparency, and compliance with regulatory requirements.

Boards of directors and senior management are responsible for establishing a robust liquidity risk management framework, allocating sufficient resources, and providing oversight of liquidity risk-taking activities.

By adopting comprehensive liquidity risk management practices, banks can enhance their ability to withstand liquidity shocks, maintain market confidence, and sustain their operations and financial stability over the long term.

Asset Liability Management

Asset Liability Management (ALM) is a strategic management process used by financial institutions, such as banks, to effectively manage their balance sheet in order to optimize risk and return. ALM involves matching the maturity, liquidity, and interest rate characteristics of a bank's assets and liabilities to minimize the risk of funding mismatches and maximize profitability. Here's an overview of the key components and objectives of ALM:

Assets: Assets represent the investments and earning assets held by a financial institution, including loans, securities, investments, and other income-generating assets. ALM focuses on managing the composition, quality, and performance of these assets to optimize returns while controlling risks.

Liabilities: Liabilities represent the sources of funding for a financial institution, including deposits, borrowings, and other liabilities. ALM involves managing the cost, structure, and maturity profile of these liabilities to ensure adequate funding and liquidity to support the bank's asset portfolio.

Interest Rate Risk: Interest rate risk arises from fluctuations in interest rates that can affect the profitability and value of a bank's assets and liabilities. ALM aims to manage interest rate risk by aligning the interest rate sensitivity of assets and liabilities, using techniques such as duration gap analysis, income gap analysis, and scenario analysis.

Liquidity Risk: Liquidity risk refers to the risk of not being able to meet short-term funding obligations or liquidate assets at a reasonable price. ALM focuses on maintaining sufficient liquidity buffers and contingency funding sources to meet liquidity needs under various market conditions and stress scenarios.

Funding Strategies: ALM involves developing funding strategies that balance the cost, stability, and flexibility of funding sources, such as deposits, wholesale funding, and capital instruments. These strategies aim to optimize funding costs while ensuring reliable access to funding to support business operations and growth.

Capital Management: ALM considers the capital adequacy and efficiency of a financial institution's capital structure, including regulatory capital requirements and capital ratios. It involves managing capital allocation, capital planning, and capital optimization strategies to support business activities and absorb unexpected losses.

Risk Measurement and Monitoring: ALM employs risk measurement and monitoring tools to assess and monitor various risks, such as interest rate risk, liquidity risk, credit risk, and market risk. These tools help identify potential risks, evaluate their impact on the balance sheet, and implement risk mitigation strategies as needed.

Risk Management: The primary objective of ALM is to manage and mitigate risks associated with interest rate fluctuations, liquidity constraints, credit exposures, and other market dynamics. By aligning the maturity, liquidity, and interest rate profiles of assets and liabilities, ALM helps minimize funding mismatches and reduce the bank's vulnerability to adverse market conditions.

Profitability Optimization: ALM aims to optimize the profitability of a financial institution by maximizing net interest income, net interest margin, and overall returns on assets and equity. This involves balancing the yield and risk characteristics of assets and liabilities to achieve a sustainable and competitive level of profitability.

Capital Preservation: ALM seeks to preserve and enhance the capital position of a financial institution by ensuring adequate capital buffers, maintaining capital ratios above regulatory requirements, and managing capital efficiently to support business growth and risk-taking activities.

Compliance and Regulatory Requirements: ALM ensures compliance with regulatory requirements and industry standards related to capital adequacy, liquidity management, risk management, and financial reporting. It involves adhering to regulatory guidelines, conducting stress tests, and preparing for regulatory examinations and audits.

Strategic Decision-Making: ALM provides valuable insights and inputs for strategic decision-making, including asset allocation, funding strategies, product pricing, and business expansion initiatives. By integrating ALM considerations into strategic planning processes, financial institutions can align their business objectives with risk management priorities and long-term sustainability goals.

Overall, Asset Liability Management is a holistic approach to managing the balance sheet of financial institutions, encompassing risk management, profitability optimization, capital preservation, and strategic decision-making to ensure the stability, resilience, and profitability of the institution in a dynamic and evolving financial environment.

E-Payment System

It's a payment mechanism which enables individuals, businesses, government and nonprofit organizations to make cashless payments for goods and services through cards, mobile phones over the internet. Examples: payment through debit card, credit card, smart card, net banking etc. An electronic payment system is a technologically-driven platform that enables the transfer of funds electronically, allowing individuals and businesses to make online transactions securely and conveniently. It leverages various digital channels, such as credit/debit cards, mobile wallets, internet banking, electronic funds transfers (EFTs), and crypto currency, to facilitate seamless money exchanges.

Benefits of using electronic payment methods?

Convenience: Electronic payment methods offer users the ease of conducting transactions anytime and anywhere, reducing the reliance on physical cash or checks.

Speed: Payments made through electronic systems are processed instantly, enabling swift and immediate fund transfers, enhancing business operations and customer satisfaction.

Security: Robust encryption and authentication mechanisms in electronic payment systems protect financial data, reducing the risk of fraud and unauthorized access.

Cost-Effectiveness: Electronic payments often entail lower processing fees than traditional payment methods, leading to cost savings for businesses and consumers.

Enhanced Record-Keeping: Digital payment systems maintain detailed transaction records, facilitating better financial tracking and reporting for businesses and individuals.

Global Accessibility: With electronic payment systems, cross-border transactions become seamless, promoting international trade and enabling businesses to reach a global customer base.

Eco-Friendly: By reducing the need for paper-based transactions, electronic payment methods contribute to environmental sustainability and reduce paper waste.

Contactless Options: The rise of contactless payment technologies offers hygienic and secure payment alternatives, especially in the context of public health concerns.

Disadvantages and Risks of Electronic Payment

Security Risks: Despite strong security measures, electronic payment systems are vulnerable to hacking, data breaches, and identity theft, potentially exposing customers' sensitive information.

Technical Glitches: System failures or technical glitches in electronic payment platforms can disrupt transactions and cause inconvenience to both businesses and customers.

Dependency on Technology: Electronic payment systems heavily rely on technology and the internet. Any disruption in network connectivity or power outage can disrupt payment services.

Fraud and Scams: Cybercriminals continuously develop new methods to exploit vulnerabilities in electronic payment systems, leading to fraudulent activities that can harm businesses and individuals.

Lack of Anonymity: Electronic transactions leave digital footprints, compromising user privacy and anonymity compared to cash transactions.

Potential Fees: While electronic payments are generally cost-effective, some transactions may incur additional fees, especially for cross-border transactions or currency conversions.

Limited Acceptance: In some regions or certain demographics, electronic payment methods may have limited acceptance, which can inconvenience users who prefer or rely on traditional payment methods.

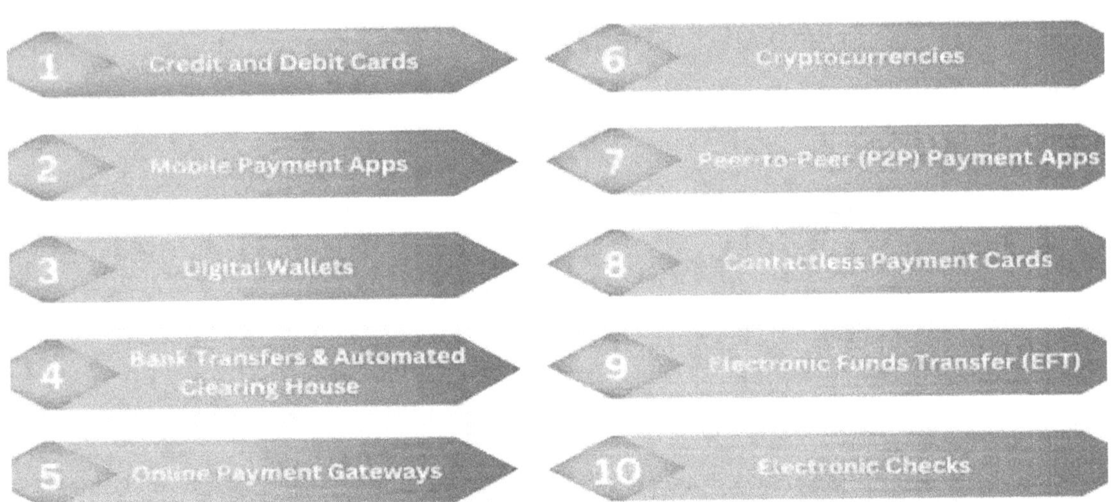


Debit Card: A debit card is a card with unique credentials and is linked to the customer's bank account. A debit card deducts money from the user's bank account instantly at the time of the transaction – which is the main distinction between a debit card and a credit card.

Credit Cards: Credit cards are the most popular form of payment for e-commerce transactions. Enabling credit card payments on your website can enable customers to shop without having to worry about paying upfront.

E-Wallet: The E-Wallet can be thought of as a prepaid account that enables users to store a information each time, thus promoting a rapid checkout. PhonePe, PayTM, Mobikwik, Amazon Pay, etc are some of the well-known digital or E-wallets in India.

Smart Card: In terms of appearance, debit/credit cards and smart cards are somewhat comparable. Smart cards, however, contain an embedded microprocessor chip. It has the ability to store money as well as a person's personal and professional information. Faster processing is possible with smart cards at lower rates.

Online banking: Customers can conveniently make purchases by paying with a bank account directly. The user does not need a debit card to use this e-commerce payment system, but they still need to register with their bank for a net banking facility. The customer only needs to provide their net banking ID and PIN in order to complete a purchase.

Mobile Payment: Customers may easily and quickly use mobile payment to make purchases using their smart phones. A user only needs to download a mobile payment app from the applications store. They must then link their bank account to that app in order to add money to their wallet and make purchases, as well as to make payments directly from their bank account. When a consumer chooses to use that app to pay on an e-commerce website, the app receives a payment request, which it must approve before the payment can be processed.

Considerations for Businesses Adopting Electronic Payments:

Cost and Fee Structures

Before adopting electronic payment methods, businesses must assess the associated costs and fee structures. Different payment providers may have varying transaction fees, processing charges, and setup costs. It's crucial to compare options to ensure cost-effectiveness and alignment with the company's budget.

Integration with Accounting Systems

Seamless integration with existing accounting systems is essential for efficient financial management. Businesses should opt for electronic payment solutions that integrate smoothly with their accounting software to automate reconciliation, streamline bookkeeping, and enhance accuracy in financial reporting.

Customer Support and Dispute Resolution

Businesses must consider the level of customer support the payment service provider provides. Timely and effective customer support is critical for resolving any issues that customers may encounter during the payment process. A clear dispute resolution mechanism also helps address payment disputes efficiently, minimizing customer dissatisfaction.

Regulatory Compliance and Data Privacy

Adherence to regulatory requirements and data privacy laws is non-negotiable. Businesses must ensure that the chosen electronic payment system complies with relevant regulations and safeguards sensitive customer data. Compliance helps build trust with customers and avoids potential legal liabilities.

Electronic Payments Work – A step-by-step guide

How Electronic Payments Work: A Step-by-Step Guide

Authorization and Authentication Process

When a customer initiates an electronic payment, the process begins with the authorization and authentication step. The customer provides their payment information, such as credit/debit card details, through a secure online platform or a payment app. The payment system then verifies the authenticity of the customer's information by conducting various security checks, including card verification; address verification, and sometimes multi-factor authentication for added security.

Transaction Settlement and Clearing

After the payment is authorized, the transaction enters the settlement and clearing phase. During this stage, the payment details are sent to the acquiring bank (merchant's bank) and the issuing bank (customer's bank). The acquiring bank forwards the payment request to the payment network (e.g., Visa, MasterCard, or other payment processors). The payment network then communicates with the issuing bank to verify the customer's account details and available funds.

Encryption and Secure Transmission

Throughout the entire electronic payment process, data security is paramount. All sensitive information, including card numbers and personal details, is encrypted to protect it from unauthorized access during transmission. SSL (Secure Sockets Layer) or TLS (Transport Layer Security) protocols are commonly used to encrypt data, ensuring it remains secure as it travels between the customer's device, the merchant's server, and the payment gateway.

Payment Gateways and Processors

The payment gateway is an intermediary between the merchant's website/app and the payment networks. It securely transmits the customer's payment data to the payment processor for further processing. The payment processor's role is to facilitate the actual fund transfer between the customer's and merchant's banks. It validates the transaction and ensures that the funds are transferred accurately and securely.

Transaction Completion and Notification

Once the payment processor confirms the successful completion of the transaction, a confirmation message is sent to the payment gateway. The payment gateway then communicates this information to the merchant's system, confirming the successful payment. The merchant can proceed to fulfill the customer's order or provide the desired service.

INSURANCE

Introduction Definition: It is a form of contract or agreement which one party agrees in return of a consideration to pay an agreed amount of money to another party to make good for a loss, damage, injury to something of value in which the insured has to pay as a result of some uncertain event. Thus, insurance is a method of securing protection against future calamities and uncertainties.

Advantages of Insurance:

Provide certainty: Insurance helps the insured to convert his uncertainties into certainties by entering into contract with insurer. The payment of premium by insured enables to reduce the risk.

Distribution of losses: It helps to distribute the losses as it enables to transfer the risks and spread the financial loss of insured members over the whole insurers.

Social security: It acts as an instrument to fight against evils of poverty, unemployment, disease, old age, accidents, fire and other calamities.

Credit facility: The policies issued by insurance companies can be made use to raise policy loans from insurance company, as well traders are in the position to raise loans and get credit facilities from various financial institutions.

Increase efficiency: It reduces the risk and increases the efficiency in business. It provides security for business community which in turn paves the way for growth and diversification of the industry.

Earns foreign exchange: It provides security to the international traders, shippers and banking institutions, thus paves the way for expansion of foreign trade. The increased foreign trade activities lead to securing foreign exchange which makes the country to become economically strong.

Principles of Insurance:

Insurable interest: the person getting an insurance policy must have insurable interest in the property or life insured. A person said to have an insurable interest if he is financially benefited by the existence property and is prejudiced by its loss.

Utmost good faith: faith refers to absence of fraud on the part of the parties to the contract. The insured should disclose all the material facts to the insurer. If utmost good faith is lacking the contracts made by the parties becomes invalid.

Indemnity: the principles are applied to all the insurance contracts where the loss suffered by the insured can be measured in monetary value. Hence all the contract of insurance, expect life insurance are the contracts of indemnity bcoz loss of life cannot be measured in terms of money.

Proximate cause: it is also called as causa proxima which means nearest or proximate or immediate cause. This principle is useful in deciding the actual cause of loss when a number of causes have contributed for the occurrence of loss.

Subrogation: it is also known as Doctrine of Rights Substitution. The insurer will step into the shoes of the insured and become entitled to all rights of action against the third party to cover the loss.

Contribution: this principle ensures equitable distribution of losses among the insurers. The total loss suffered by the insured is contributed by all insures in the ratio of the value of policies issued by them for same subject matter.

Mitigation of loss: it says that duty of the insured is to take all such steps to minimize the loss as would have been taken by any person who is not insured. Re-insurance: It refers to an insurance contract between two or more insurance companies. Every insurer undertakes to bear the risk according to his capacity. In order to safe guard his interest. he may insure the same risk undertaken by him along with another insurer. Hence it is a contract between two insurance companies' i.e. first insurer and reinsurer.

Objectives of Re-insurance:

To safeguard the interest of insurers by wider distribution of risks
To limit the liability of insurer and to keep him in permissible limits of financial capacity.
To stabilize the underwritings over a period of time.
To help in steady accumulation of reserves by the insurer.
To safeguard against serious effects of uncertainties.

Insurance Regulatory & Development Authority (IRDA) Act 1999.
The IRDA is a corporate body. With LPG many private companies are being permitted to transact insurance business in India. It is advise by an insurance advisory committee consisting of more than 25 members to represent the interests of commerce, industry,

transport, agriculture etc.

Objectives:

To establish an authority to protect the interest of the holders of the insurance policies.

To regulate, promote and ensure orderly growth of insurance industry.

To amend the related insurance acts to suit the requirements of the society Duties of authority

Orderly growth of insurance business: the important duty is to regulate, promote and ensure growth of the insurance business and re-insurance business.

Maintaining proper accounts: the authority should maintain proper accounts and other relevant records for the accounting period. It has to prepare annual statements of accounts in the prescribed form in consultation with comptroller and auditor general of India.

Rectify defects: as per the directions of the central government and comptroller and auditor general, the authority has to go for audit of the accounts and rectify the defects if any.

Submission of annual reports: the authority has to submit the audited financial accounts to the central govt to present the reports beefier the houses of the parliament.

Duration of the filing: the authority should submit the financial statements to the central govt within 9 months from the completion of financial year.

Report on promotional programs: the authority should submit report on the promotional programs undertaken for the development of insurance industry.

Protect the policy holders: they should protect the interest of policyholders with regard to assignment of policy, nomination, claims settlement, surrender value etc.

Powers & functions of authority: 1. It has general supervisory power of insurance industry

It has administrative power to appoint the staff required for the conduct of its business

It has power to prepare code of conduct for the agents, surveyors or other intermediaries who took part in the insurance business.

It promotes efficiency.

It has the power to levy fees and other charges for providing services to the insures

It has the power to regulate the investment of funds by insurance companies

It can exercise the powers sanctioned by insurance laws and central government from time to time.

It has the power to check the functioning of tariff advisory committee

It has the power to regulate the margin of insolvency.

It has a power to issue of registration, renew, modify, withdraw, suspend or cancel the registration of insures.

It has the power to call for the information from insurance companies, to inspect the records, conduct enquires and call for explanation. Ombudsperson: An ombudsman is an official, usually appointed by the government, who investigates complaints against businesses, financial institutions, or government departments or other public entities, and attempts to resolve the conflicts or concerns raised, either by mediation or by making recommendations.

LIFE INSURANCE

Meaning/ Definition: Life insurance is a contract in which one party agrees to pay given sum on the happening of a particular event contingent upon the duration of the human life in consideration of the immediate payment of a smaller sum or certain equivalent periodical payments by another.

Procedure for issuing life insurance policy:

Proposal for insurance policy: The person intending to take an insurance policy has to make a written requisition in the prescribed form to the insurance company. The insured has to provide information on various aspects such as name, occupation, address, mode of payment, sum assured, etc. The insured should provide true and correct information to the insurance company otherwise the contract cannot be enforceable.

Providing proof of age: The proposer has to give proof of his age along with proposal form if the age is less than 25 yrs and more than 50 yrs. However if the age is ranging between 25 to 50 he need not submit the proof of his age.

Undergoing medical examination: The proposal form is sent to the doctor for approval. The insured has to appear for the medical examination. The doctor examines the proposer's health condition and prepares a report which is sent to the insurance company.

Confidential report of the agent: After the medical report is received, agent is required to furnish a confidential report about the proposer in prescribed form. The report contains true info about the proposer i.e health condition, financial position, reputation etc.

Acceptance of proposal: the insurance company determines type of risk, volume of risk, premium rate etc and if the assessment is favorable, insurer accepts the proposal.

Payment of first premium: on receiving the acceptance letter the proposer has to pay the first premium within the time stipulated. Once the first premium paid by the insured, the insurer becomes liable from the day on which it is paid. Premium may be paid monthly, quarterly, and half yearly.

Preparing and issuing insurance policy: once the premium receipt issue by the insurance company, the policy comes into operation and risk is covered from that date only. Issue of duplicate policy: It is the duty of the insured to safeguard the original policy but it might misplace due to certain reasons such as theft. Fire etc. if the policy is in force and not matured the policyholder may ask for duplicate policy. The insurer has to verify the reasons under which the policy is lost. The insurer has to obtain an indemnity bond duly signed by the policy holder and surety. The insurer should verify whether FIR is filed in PS in case of loss of policy by theft. After satisfying all the formalities a new document is issued. A rubber stamp indicating Duplicate may be affixed on the new policy document. The insured has to bear the costs of issue of duplicate policy, stamp duty etc. Nomination: The insured who takes the life insurance policy nominate the person or person to whom the money secured by the policy shall be paid in the event of the death.

The insured may nominate a person to whom the policy shall be paid in the event of the death.

Any change in the name of nominee must be communicated by insured to the insurer within a written notice

If the nominee dies before the policy matures the amount is paid to the policy holder and if he too expires the amount is paid to the legal representatives of insured. Surrender value: it is a voluntary termination of the contract by the policy holder. The policy holder can surrender the policy at any time before it becomes a claim. The amount payable by insurer to the insured on the surrender policy is called as surrender value. It is calculated on the basis of actual premium paid and the no.of yrs of the policy are in force. The minimum period required for surrender value in LIC is 3 yrs. Policy loan: Availability of loan on the security of the policy is an important privilege to the policy holder. Loans are generally granted up to 90% of the surrender value for the policies in force and 85% of surrender value for paid up policies. The rate of interest charged on policy loans is 9.5 % p.a. for getting the policy loan the policy holder has to assign the policy to the insurer company. The policy holder has to make interest payment on due date otherwise interest is added to the principal amount. If the loan amount is not paid and interest is not paid and when policy becomes claim i.e either death or maturity the outstanding amount is deducted and balance is only paid to the insured. Assignment: the general meaning of assignment is transfer of property means an act by which a living person conveys property, in present send in future to one or more living person. The term living person includes a company or association or body of individuals whether incorporated or not.

Features of Assignment:

An assignment is actionable claim and empowers the policy holder to sell, mortgage, charge or gift the policy to any person of his interest.

An assignment must be signed by the transferor or his duty authorized agent.

The assignor must be major and competent to contract.

The signature of the policy holder must be attested by witness.

An assignment must be sent to the insurer along with a notice. If assignment is not delivered to the insurer, it does not come into force.

Claims settlement:

Maturity claim: A maturity claim is payable to the insured as per the terms of the contract at the end of the policy period, if he lives up to that date. Insurer informs to the policy holder about the maturity policy and insured should submit the policy documents, age of proof if it is not admitted and the stamped document of assignment if it is assigned. After receiving the documents the insurer has to initiate action for making payment and settlement of claims. Before making the payment the insurer has to verify the age proof, all the premiums are paid or not, original policy is surrendered etc. and then the payment is made to the policy holder.

Death claims: It is a claim that arises out of death which may be a natural, a suicide or an accidental on. Insurer has to make enquiry about the genuineness of the claim. To claim the amount the insurer should the claimant to submit the relevant documents such as name of policy holder, place, date, cause, time of death, name of the doctor who treated for illness, etc.

Death claim has following procedure: a. Intimation of death: when the policy holder is dead the intimation must be given to the insurer.
Filling up claim form: the claimant should fill up all the details in the form given by the insurer.

Proof of death: the claimant has to provide the death certificate obtained from the municipality, Panchayath or doctor.

Proof of claimant: the person claiming the policy must satisfy the insurer that he is the legal representative or nominee of the insured.
Submission of original policy: the claimant ha to submit the original policy document to the insurer and duplicate policy in case when original document is lost.

Accident and disablement claims: the death may occur due to accident or disablement. The insurer must be very careful before making the payment. The insurer has to ensure that all the conditions are satisfied or not.

The conditions for making payment for self-accident benefits are:

a. The accident should be unintentional one b. The death must be result of injuries caused by the accident c. The death must occur within 120 days or such other period is specified.

d. The claimant has to intimate about the death as a result of the accident and should produce the evidence to the insurer. The following documents are to be submitted: a.
FIR b. Postmortem report

c. Hospital reports etc. Disability claim: It refers to the loss of sight, amputation of hands, legs etc. The conditions for claiming the disability benefits are: a. The disability must be permanent

b. It must result before the assured attain the age of 65 yrs. Once all the documents are submitted to the insurer and if he is satisfied the insured will get an additional sum equal to the sum assured is paid in monthly installments over 10 yrs the premium is allowed from the date followed by the accident which resulted in disability.

Survival benefit claims: Insurance companies offer some policies in which the policy holder is entitled for the survival benefit before the expiry of the full term policy like money back policy. The procedure for settlement of benefit claim are:

The insurer gives advance intimation about the survival benefit along with discharge voucher. The insured has to return the discharge voucher filled, stamped and signed along with the signatures of witness and their address.

The net amount is payable after making necessary deductions.

NON-LIFE INSURANCE Definition: It defines as fire, marine or miscellaneous business, whether carried on singly or in combinations with one or more of them. Miscellaneous insurances include motor insurance, burglary, personal accident etc. thus the non-life insurance covers the business and other activities except the life insurance.

Types of non-life insurance products:

Commercial line of insurance

Personal line of insurance.

Commercial line of insurance

Policies for cottage, tiny and small sector industries: the policies intended to meet the requirements of the industries are burglary, cash policy, motor policy etc.

Policies for traders: the policies offered to the traders are fire policy, marine cargo policy, plate glass and neon sign insurance, shopkeeper's policy etc.

Policies for professional and specific professions insurance: The policies offered are Hull insurance, stock exchange and brokers insurance, PLG dealers' package insurance, adhikari suraksha kavach etc.

Policies fir industries and commercial organizations: the policies can be taken on the basis of project covers and operational covers.

Personal line of insurance.

Property insurance policies: the policies offered are phone insurance, gruha raksha policy, householder policy, TV policy etc.

Accident insurance policies: policies offered are personal accident policy, suhana safar policy, bhagya shri policy etc.

Health insurance policy: policies offered are mediclaim insurance, jan arogya insurance, videshi yatra mitra policy, cancer insurance etc.

Liability insurance policies: the policies offered are professional indemnity policy, doctors indemnity policy etc.

I FIRE INSURANCE: It is an agreement whereby one party in return for a consideration undertake to indemnify the other party against the financial loss for the goods damaged or destroyed by means of fire. Characteristics of fire insurance:

Contract of indemnity: The insured can only to the value of the goods damaged by fire or the amount of policy whichever is less.

Offer and acceptance: offer is made by the insured and acceptance by the insurer.

Lawful consideration: the consideration is paid by the insured which is called as premium.

Period of insurance: the policy is normally given for 1 year only. It is renewable every year on fulfillment of formalities.
Cause of accident: the loss must be the outcome of fire or ignition.

Claim for settlement: if the fire is result of fraud or misconduct on the part of insured the loss is not indemnified. But if the loss occurred due to negligence of the insured is admitted for indemnifying the loss.

**Scope of fire insurance:**

Ordinary scope: firstly there must be actual fir or ignition and secondly the fire must be accidental and unintentional. Normally risks such as fire or ignition, blasting of gas cylinders for household purpose, used for lighting and heating in any building are covered under fire insurance. Goods and properties like precious stones, stamps, cheques , books etc and loss caused by events like earthquakes , cyclones, floods etc are not covered under fire insurance.

Broader scope: these special fire insurance policies my cover the risks excluded from ordinary scope of fire insurance such as perils and risk. II MARINE INURANCE: Marine insurance is an agreement by which the insurance company or the underwriter agrees to indemnify the owner of the ship or cargo against the risk involved in marine cargo and ship. It covers a large no. of risks such as sinking of ship, burning of ship, sea dacoits, stormy winds etc.

Characteristics of Marine Insurance:

Consideration: insured us under obligation to pay certain amount periodically to the insurer in consideration for accepting the risk.

Coverage of insurance: In marine insurance cargo, ship and freight can be insured.

Mode of insurance: the insurance may be for single journey or number of journeys or for specific period of time.

Condition for compensation: insure dis compensated only when the loss is occurred to the ship or cargo. It also includes third party insurance.

Scope for marine insurance:

Hull insurance: insuring the ship against the risks of sea transportation is called as hull insurance. It is exposed to various risks such as sinking, burning, collision, explosion etc.

Cargo insurance: the term cargo refers to goods carried in a ship in the course of shipment. The insurance which covers the risk such as fire, gales perils etc. is called as cargo insurance, any loss incurred to cargo during transportation from one port to another is indemnified by the insurance company.

Freight insurance: freight refers to payment received for the transportation of goods. The policy is taken by freight receiver to protect freight purchases. If the ship fails to reach the destination due to marine perils, the freight receiver losses the freight.

## INTRODUCTION OF INDIAN FINANCIAL SYSTEM

Meaning of Indian financial system
The financial system enables lenders and borrowers to exchange funds. India has a financial system that is controlled by independent regulators in the sectors of insurance, banking, capital markets and various services sectors.

Thus, a financial system can be said to play a significant role in the economic growth of a country by mobilizing the surplus funds and utilizing them effectively for productive purposes.

## FEATURES OF INDIAN FINANCIAL SYSTEM:

- It plays a vital role in economic development of a country.

- It encourages both savings and investment.

- It links savers and investors.

- It helps in capital formation.

- It helps in allocation of risk.

- It facilitates expansion of financial markets.

## COMPONENTS/ CONSTITUENTS OF INDIAN FINANCIAL SYSTEM

The following are the four major components that comprise the Indian Financial System:

1. Financial Institutions

2. Financial Markets

3. Financial Instruments/ Assets/ Securities

*4.* Financial Services.

COMPONENT IS DISCUSSED BELOW:
FINANCIAL INSTITUTIONS

Financial institutions are intermediaries that facilitate the smooth functioning of the financial system by creating a meeting between investors and borrowers. They hold the accumulation of surplus units and allocate them to productive activity that guarantees better returns. Financial institutions also provide services to entities (private, business, government) seeking advice on a variety of issues, from restructuring to diversification plans. They provide a whole range of services to entities that want to raise funds from the markets or from other venues.

Financial institutions are also termed as financial intermediaries because they act as middle between savers by accumulating Funds them and borrowers by lending these fund.

It is also act as intermediaries because they accept deposits from a set of customers (savers lend these funds to another set of customers (borrowers). Like - wise investing institutions such ICCIC, mutual funds also accumulate savings and lend these to borrowers, thus perform the role of financial intermediaries.


TYPES OF FINANCIAL INSTITUTIONS

Financial institutions can be classified into two categories:

*A.* Banking Institutions

*B.* Non - Banking Financial Institutions

## A. BANKING INSTITUTIONS (Reserve Bank of India)

The Indian banking industry is regulated by the central bank. As the apex institution, the Reserve Bank of India controls, operates, supervises, controls and develops the monetary and financial system of the country. The main law governing commercial banking in India is the Banking Act, 1949.

The Indian banking institutions can be broadly classified into two categories:

*1.* Organised Sector

*2.* Unorganized Sector.

*1.* Organised  Sector

The organised banking sector consists of commercial banks, cooperative banks and the regional rural banks.

*(a)* Commercial Banks: The commercial banks may be scheduled banks or non – scheduled banks. At present only one bank is a non - scheduled hank. All other banks are schedule banks. The commercial banks consist of 27 public sector banks, private sector banks and foreign banks. Prior to 1969, all major banks with the exception of State Bank of India in the private sector. An important step towards public sector banking was taken in July 1969, when 14 major private banks with a deposit base of 50 crores or more were nationalised. Later in 1980 another 6 were nationalised bringing up the total number banks nationalised to twenty.

*(b)* Co-operative banks: An important segment of the organized sector of Indian banking is the co-operative banking. The segment is represented by a group of societies registered under the Acts of the states relating to co- operative societies. In fact, co-operative societies may be credit societies

or non-credit societies.

Different types of co-operative credit societies are operating in Indian economy. These institutions can be classified into two broad categories:
(a) Rural credit societies which are primary agriculture, (b) Urban credit societies which are primarily non-agriculture.

For the purpose of agriculture credit there are different co-operative credit institutions to meet different kinds of needs.

*(c)* Regional Rural Banks (RRBs): Regional Rural Banks were set by the state government and sponsoring commercial banks with the objective of developing the rural economy. Regional rural banks provide banking services and credit to small farmers, small entrepreneurs in the rural areas. The regional rural banks were set up with a view to provide credit facilities to weaker sections. They constitute an important part of the rural financial architecture in India. There were 196 RRBs at the end of June 2002, as compares to 107 in 1981 and 6 in 1975.

*(d)* Foreign Banks: Foreign banks have been in India from British days. Foreign banks as banks that have branches in the other countries and main Head Quarter in the Home Country. With the deregulation (Elimination of Government Authority) in 1993, a number of foreign banks are entering India.                                              Foreign Banks
are: Citi Bank. Bank of Ceylon.

*2.* Unorganised Sector.

In the unorganised banking sector are the Indigenous Bankers, Money Lenders.

*1.* Indigenous Bankers

Indigenous Bankers are private firms or individual who operate as banks and as such both receive deposits and given loans. Like bankers, they also financial intermediaries. They should be distinguished professional money lenders whose primary business is not banking and money lending. The indigenous banks are trading with the Hundies, Commercial Paper.

*1.* Money Lenders:

Money lenders depend entirely to on their one funds. Money Lenders may be rural or urban, professional or non-professional. They include large number of farmer, merchants, traders. Their operations are entirely unregulated. They charge very high rate of interst.

B. NON - BANKING  INSTITUTIONS

The non - banking institutions may be categorized broadly into two groups:

*(a)* Organised Non - Banking Financial Institutions.

*(b)* Unorganised Non - Banking Financial Institutions.

*(a)* Organised Non - Banking Financial Institutions

The organised non - banking financial institutions include:

1. Development Finance Institutions.

These include: The institutions like IDBT, ICICI, IFCI, IIBI, IRDC at all India level. The State Finance Corporations (SFCs), State Industrial Development Corporations (SIDCs) at the state level. Agriculture Development Finance Institutions as NABARD, LDBS etc. Development banks provide medium and long term finance to the corporate and industrial sector and also take up promotional activities for economic development

2. Investment Institutions.

These include those financial institutions which mobilise savings at the public at large through various schemes and invest these funds in corporate and government securities. These include LIC, GIC, LTT, and mutual funds.

The non - banking financial institutions in the organised sector) have been discussed at length in detail in separate chapters of this book.

**(b)** Unorganised Non - Banking Financial Institutions:
The unorganised non - banking financial institutions include number of non
- banking financial companies (NBFCs) providing whole range of financial services. These include hire - purchase 300 consumer finance companies, leasing companies, housing finance companies, factoring companies, Credit rating agencies, merchant banking companies etc. NBFCs mobilise public funds and provide loanable funds.

## FINANCIAL MARKET

It is through financial markets and institutions that the financial system of an economic works. Financial markets refer to the institutional arrangements for dealing in financial assets and credit instruments of different types such as currency, cheques, bank deposits, bills, bonds etc.

Functions of financial markets are:

*(i)* To facilitate creation and allocation of credit and liquidity

*(ii)* To serve as intermediaries for mobilisaton of savings.

*(iii)* To assist the process of balanced economic growth.

*(iv)* To provide financial convenience.

*(v)* To cater to the various credit needs of the business houses.

they are

se organised markets can be further classified into two

*(i)* Capital Market

*(ii)* Money Market

## CAPITAL MARKET

The capital market is a market for financial assets which have a long or indefinite maturity. Generally, it deals with long term securities which have a maturity period of above one year. Capital market may be further divided into three namely:

*(I)* Industrial securities market

*(II)* Government securities market and

*(III)* Long term loans market

## *1.* INDUSTRIAL SECURITIES MARKET:

As the very name implies, it is a market for industrial securities namely:

*(i)* Equity shares or ordinary shares,

*(ii)* Preference shares and

*(iii)* Debentures or bonds.

It is a market where industrial concerns raise their capital or debt by issuing appropriate instruments. It can be further subdivided into two. They are:

*(i)* Primary market or New issue market

*(ii)* Secondary market or Stock exchange

Primary Market

Primary market is a market for new issues or new financial claims. Hence, it is also called New Issue market. The primary market deals with those securities which are issued to the public for the first time.

In the primary market, borrowers exchange new financial securities for long term funds. Thus, primary market facilitates capital formation. There are three ways by which a company may raise capital in a primary market. They are:

*(i)* Public issue

*(ii)* Rights issue

*(iii)* Private placement

The most common method of raising capital by new companies is through sale of securities to the public. It is called public issue. When an existing company wants to raise additional capital, securities are first offered to the existing shareholders on a pre-emptive basis. It is called rights issue.
Private placement is a way of selling securities privately to a small group of investors.

## Secondary Market

Secondary market is a market for secondary sale of securities. In other words, securities which have already passed through the new issue market are traded in this market. Generally, such securities are quoted the Stock Exchange and it provides a continuous and regular market to buying and selling of securities. This market consists of all stock exchanges recognised by the Government of India. The stock exchanges in India are regulated under the Securities Contracts (Regulation) Act 1956. The Bombay Stock Exchange is the principal stock exchange in India which sets the tone of the other stock markets.

## II. GOVERNMENT SECURITIES MARKET

It is otherwise called Gilt - Edged securities market. It is a market where Government securities are traded. In India there are many kinds of Government Securities - short term and long term. Long term securities are traded in this market while short term securities are traded in the money market. Securities issued by the Central Government, State Governments, Semi Government authorities like City Corporations, Port Trusts etc. Improvement Trusts, State Electricity Boards, All India and State level financial institutions and public sector enterprises are dealt in this market.

## III. LONG TERM LOANS MARKET

Development banks and commercial banks play a significant role in this market by supplying long term loans to corporate customers. Long term loans market may

further be classified into:

(1) Term loans market

*(ii)* Mortgages market

*(iii)* Financial Guarantees market.

## Term Loans Market

In India, many industrial financing institutions have been created by the Government both at the national and regional levels to supply long term and medium term loans to corporate customers directly as well as indirectly. These development banks dominate the industrial finance in India. Institutions like IDBI, IFCI, ICICI, and other financial corporations come under this category.

## Mortgages Market

A mortgage loan is a loan against the security of immovable property like real estate. The transfer of interest in a specific immovable property to secure a loan is called mortgage. This mortgage may be equitable mortgage or legal one.

## MONEY MARKET

Money market is a market for dealing with financial assets and securities which have a maturity period of upto one year. In other words, it is a market for purely short term funds. The money market may be subdivided into four. They are:

*(i)* Call money market

*(ii)* Commercial bills market

*(iii)* Treasury bilis market

*(iv)* Short term loan market. Call

Money Market

The call money market is a market for extremely short period loans say one day to fourteen days. So, it is highly liquid. The loans are repayable on demand at the option of either the lender or the borrower. In India, call money markets are associated with the presence of stock exchanges and hence, they are located in major industrial towns like Bombay, Calcutta, Madras, Delhi, Ahmedabad etc. The special feature of this market is that the interest rate varies from day to day and even from hour to hour and centre to centre. It is very sensitive to changes in demand and supply of call loans.

Commercial Bills Market

It is a market for Bills of Exchange arising out of genuine trade transactions. In the case of credit sale, the seller may draw a bill of exchange on the buyer. The buyer accepts such a bill promising to pay at a later date specified in the bill. The seller need not wait until the due date of the bill. Instead, he can get immediate payment by discounting the bill.

Treasury Bills Market

It is a market for treasury bills which have ' short - term ' maturity. A treasury bill is a promissory note or a finance bill issued by the Government.

It is highly liquid because its repayment is guaranteed by the Government. It is an important instrument for short term borrowing of the Government There are two types of treasury bills namely (i) ordinary or regular and (ii) ad hoc treasury bills popularly known as ' ad hocs'. Ordinary treasury bills are issued to the public, banks and other financial institutions with a view to raising resources for the Central Government to meet its short term financial needs. Ad hoc treasury bills are issued in favour of the RBI only.

They are not sold through tender or auction. They can be purchased by the RBI only.      Ad hocs are not marketable in India but holders of these bills can sell them back to RBI.

Short - Term Loan Market

It is a market where short - term loans are given to corporate customers for meeting their working capital requirements. Commercial banks play a significant role in this market. Commercial banks provide short term loans in the form of cash credit and overdraft Over draft facility is mainly given to business people whereas cash credit is given to industrialists. Overdraft is purely a temporary accommodation and it is given in the current account itself. But cash credit is for a period of one year and it is sanctioned in a separate account.

*(v)*

www.ingramcontent.com/pod-product-compliance
Lightning Source LLC
Chambersburg PA
CBHW080843160726
47999CB00009B/2995